Werner Me

Beekeeping

A Practical Guide for the Novice Beekeeper
Buying Bees, Management, Rearing, Honey Production
Special Section: The Beekeeper's Yearly Work Cycle

With Color Photos by Outstanding Animal and Nature
Photographers and Drawings by Walter Berghoff

Advisory Editor: Matthew M. Vriends, PhD

English translation © Copyright 1989
by Barron's Educational Series, Inc.

© Copyright 1986 by Gräfe and Unzer
GmbH, Munich, West Germany
The title of the German book is *Bienenhaltung*

Translated from the German by Rita and Robert Kimber

All inquiries should be addressd to:
Barron's Educational Series, Inc.
250 Wireless Boulevard
Hauppauge, NY 11788

Library of Congress Catalog Card No. 88–8053

International Standard Book No. 0-8120-4089-9

Library of Congress Cataloging-in-Publication Data

Melzer, Werner, 1927–
    Beekeeping: a practical guide for the novice
Translation of: Bienenhaltung.
Includes index
1. Bee culture 2. Honeybee. I. Berghoff, Walter.
II. Vriends, Matthew M., 1937–   . III. Title.
SF523.M2513 1989   638'.1   88–8053
ISBN 0–8210–4089–9

Printed and Bound in Hong Kong
2 4900 98765432

The color photos on the covers show:
Front cover: Removing full combs for honey extraction.
Inside front cover: A swarm of honeybees made up of
about 25,000 bees (about 5½ pounds [2.5 kg]).
Inside back cover: Uncapped combs in a comb carousel.
This type of extractor is used in commercial apiaries.
Back cover, above, left: Honeybee on a sage blossom.
Above, right: Combs filled with honey.
Below, left: A marked queen with her attendants; the
queen is laying an egg in the bottom of a cell.

Below, right: A bee with pollen pellets.
Photographers:
König: Back cover, above, right; Melzer: pages 18, 56
(above, below, right); Müller: page 37 (below, left); Pflet-
schinger: pages 28 (above, right and left; below, right), 55
(above, left, and below, right), inside back cover, back
cover (below, left); Reupert: page 27 (below); Schrempp:
page 55 (above, right); Staufer: page 17; Waltenberger:
front cover, inside front cover, pages 27 (above), 28
(below, right), 38, 55 (below, left), 56 (below, left), back
cover (above, left, and below, right); Wittenkindt: page
37 (above and below, right).

Important Note and Warning
This book is aimed at the novice beekeeper who is not yet
skilled at handling bees. Anyone intending to keep bees
should first work with an established apiarist and should
also join a beekeepers' association.
An aspiring beekeeper should also take the precaution of
undergoing tests for allergies to bees or bee stings, and the
test results should determine whether or not to proceed
any further. When dealing with bees, wearing the right
clothes is as important as proper handling of the colony.
This book recommends starting out with gentle bees. But
bee stings cannot be avoided altogether. It is the respon-
sibility of the beginning beekeeper to inform himself or
herself on what to do when stung–the author's remarks on
this subject are merely recommendations.
If someone gets stung in the mouth or throat, if dizziness
or vomiting follows on being stung, or if massive stinging
causes loss of consciousness, a doctor has to be called
immediately or the victim taken to a hospital.
I should like to dedicate this book to my family and especially to my wife, staunch and enthusiastic supporters of
my beekeeping activities.

About the Author
Werner Melzer was born in 1927. From 1965 to 1983 he
was Executive Director of the German Beekeepers'
Association, whose national office in Bonn he established and headed. He also served as General Secretary
and later as Member of the Board of the German Ecological Association in Bonn. He helped found and acted, until
1985, as Executive Director and Member of the Board for
the Foundation for the Protection of Endangered Plants.
For over thirty years he has been an expert in beekeeping
and bee breeding. He is the owner of a school of practical
beekeeping and he specializes in raising queens.

Contents

Preface

Anyone who keeps bees is performing an important ecological service because many plants are dependent on bees for pollination. Of course, concern for the preservation of nature is not the only reason that more and more people are becoming interested in bees. Beekeeping is a satisfying and exciting hobby that demands that the beekeeper—to be successful—be familiar with the life cycle of bees and perform the necessary tasks at the appropriate time in the course of the changing seasons.

Beekeeping has a long tradition. It is likely that people used the products of wild bees as far back as the Bronze Age. During the Middle Ages, beekeepers, who tended wild bees that lived in hollow trees, were important because they provided both light (beeswax) and sweetener (honey). They were directly responsible to the local sovereign and were allowed to carry a crossbow to defend themselves against the honey-marauding bear. In time, these medieval beekeepers started to move the hollow trees, inclusive of bees, closer to home, and this was the beginning of apiculture.

This little handbook is designed primarily for the beginning beekeeper. In order to describe all the many tasks that have to be performed in the course of a year of beekeeping, I had to choose a simplified form of presentation, and some of my explanations may strike the more experienced reader as unusual.

I begin with a short introduction to bees, which describes the life cycle of bees and the many activities that take place inside the hive, activities that a beekeeper must understand fully to do his or her work. Then the beginner is told exactly what the necessary conditions for beekeeping are; only if these conditions are met is success with bees likely. The next chapter discusses how to choose the right kind of hives and other necessary equipment. This is followed by advice on buying, transporting, and establishing bee colonies.

Proper care and management (pages 24–43) of bees, including all the necessary manipulations, is probably the most important part of beekeeping. Anyone who does not look after the bees conscientiously is bound to suffer repeated setbacks. I have attempted to describe as lucidly as possible how to work with movable-frame hives, such as the Langstroth hives (popular in the United States), which usually accommodate 10 frames, as well as leaf hives (which are in common use in Germany). I also cover the subject of harvesting honey, starting with the removal of honeycombs from the hive and then describing how to extract and store the honey properly. Since it is often necessary to build or repair parts of the equipment oneself—where practical carpentry skills come in very handy—I have also included some instructions in this area. The chapter on the yearly work cycle (pages 46–50), in which all the chores are organized chronologically by month, should serve as a useful guide and reminder for any beekeeper but is needed especially by the novice.

The new beekeeper is also given all the necessary basic information about the different bee products and about diseases, pests, and dangers, including bee and brood diseases and damage caused by pesticides and herbicides. To aid the beginner in mastering the beekeeper's lingo quickly, a short glossary of beekeeping terms has been included. The appendix contains the addresses of beekeepers' associations and a list of books and publications for further study.

The instructive drawings and color photos will help the inexperienced beekeeper understand the activities of bees and facilitate working with them. I want to express my thanks to Mr. Walter Berghoff for his drawings and to all the photographers who have contributed their pictures, especially to Mr. Donat Waltenberger.

Werner Melzer

A Short Introduction to Bees

Division of Labor in a Honeybee Colony

Honeybees are social insects and could not survive as single organisms. In the summer a typical colony is made up of a queen, some 50,000–70,000 worker bees, and up to 2000 drones (male bees). Division of labor determines everything, and each of the three castes specializes in performing its particular tasks.

Worker   Queen   Drone

The three kinds of occupants of a beehive—worker, queen, and drone—shown in relative size. The tripartite structure (head, thorax, and abdomen) of the insects is clearly visible. Three pairs of legs are attached to the thorax and are equipped with combs and brushes used by the worker bees to brush pollen from the hair on their bodies into the pollen baskets on their hind legs. The two pairs of wings also grow from the thorax.

The queen is the sole female with fully developed ovaries. From March until October she lays between 1000 and 2000 eggs a day—under extraordinary circumstances up to 3000—an output that represents about twice her own weight. The queen also secretes a pheromone (the so-called queen substance) from the mandibular gland in her head. This scent secretion, which is taken up by the worker bees attending to the queen and passed on in minute quantities to all the bees in the hive, stimulates and inhibits certain basic behaviors and physiologic processes and thus significantly affects the life and social order of a colony.

Worker bees live only about 40 days, and the first half of their lives is spent working inside the hive, attending to the brood (see page 6). Worker bees act as nurses, build and renovate comb cells, feed the queen and drones, which are unable to feed themselves, and guard the entrance to the hive (see page 11). The young bees that work within the hive are called house or hive bees. When they are about 20 days old, they start leaving the hive to forage for nectar, honeydew, and pollen (see page 8) and are then called field or forage bees.

The sole function of drones is to mate with the virgin queen (see page 7), although their presence in the hive may also help maintain the temperature necessary for the proper development of the brood, that is, about 95°F (35°C).

Comb Building

Bees live on combs where they raise their brood and store food. The beekeeper (or apiarist) places rectangular wooden frames with thin sheets of beeswax (comb or wax foundation; see page 24) inside the hive. As soon as the house bees are 10 days old, they settle on the comb foundation and secrete wax to build, or draw, cells. The wax appears in the form of small flakes or plates between some of the segments of the bee's abdomen. It is then picked up with the mandibles and masticated before being used for the building of comb cells.

The hexagonal honeycomb pattern of the cells is embossed on the wax foundation, and this facilitates the bees' job of drawing the comb. The bees build cells on both sides of the foundation. These cells are tilted upward slightly and measure about $\frac{1}{5}$ inch (5.37 mm) across. They are used for rearing new workers and for storing honey and pollen. The bees would build cells of the right size and the same regularity without the pattern on the foundation. Having the pattern to follow saves them time, however, and also forces them to build cells exclusively for worker larvae. As the beekeeper knows very well, the more workers a colony has, the more honey there will be to harvest. In order to reproduce (see below), however, the bees must also build brood cells for drones and queen cells.

Drone cells are used not only for rearing male bees but also for the storage of honey. A queen cell, which is ¾–1¼ inches long (20–30 mm) and is shaped like a peanut or a short, blunt, icicle (see photo on page 5), is built for the exclusive purpose of rearing a new queen. After being used once as a brood cell it is demolished by the bees and carried out of the hive. Brood cells for worker bees and drones, on the other hand, are reused a number of times for raising worker and drone brood.

Reproduction

A queen lays both fertilized eggs, which develop into workers or queens, and unfertilized ones, which turn into drones. After three days, the larvae emerge from the eggs and lie curled up in their cells (see photo on page 38). Young worker bees develop brood-food glands whose secretions (brood food) are fed to the young larvae. To produce food for the larvae, the hive bees need water, which the field workers carry back to the hive in their honey stomachs and pass on to the nurse bees.

Larvae destined to become workers and drones are fed brood food only for 3½ days; after that they get a mixture of honey and pollen (see page 8). The future queen bees, however, keep getting fed secretions from the nurse bees' brood-food glands, which is why this food is called royal jelly.

The organization of the brood nest within the hive follows a pattern that makes it easy for the nurse bees to work efficiently. The queen does not fill every last cell of the comb with eggs but leaves 1 or 2 inches of empty cells at the top for the storage of honey and pollen. This way the supplies for feeding the brood are handy and the nurse bees don't have to waste much time running back and forth. When the larvae are 5 days old they start straighten-

ing out, and the nurse bees cap their cells with a wax cover. The larvae turn into nymphs, which pupate and finally develop into complete insects. The development from egg to worker bee takes 21 days. A queen takes only 16 or 17 days to develop, and drones emerge 23 or 24 days after they start life as an egg.

A crucial factor in the development of the brood is a constant temperature of 95°F (35°C) in the brood nest. Bees are heterothermic, which means that they can regulate their body temperature. If it becomes cooler outside, the bees raise the temperature inside the hive by eating more honey and converting the energy of the extra carbohydrates into increased body temperature. If the outside temperature is too warm, the bees fan the warmer air out of the hive through the entrance by rapidly beating their wings (ventilation).

A worker bee starts cleaning cells as soon as she has hatched. Her next task is to feed honey and pollen to the older larvae for a few days. She then feeds brood food to young larvae (see photo on page 38). By this time her brood-food glands, which started developing on the third day, are fully functional. Next she is assigned to relieving the field bees of their nectar, and she also cleans the hive, builds honeycomb, and guards the entrance to the hive. From day 20 until her death (at about 40 days) she is a field worker, collecting nectar and pollen. (See the chart Development and Tasks of a Worker Bee on page 12).

Ordinarily the various tasks a worker bee performs are determined by her age, but it is also possible for a field worker to take over nursing duty if there is a shortage of young hive bees. In this case her brood-food glands, which usually atrophy in field workers that have finished their nursing duties, are reactivated.

When all the cells in the hive are filled with brood and honey or pollen and there is no more comb area for the queen to lay her eggs, the worker bees suspend producing brood food. This triggers the impulse to swarm. When the bees start building queen cells, the beekeeper must initiate measures to

A Short Introduction to Bees

a Brain (upper ganglion)
b Head salivary gland
c and d Food glands in
  head (c) and thorax (d)
e Abdominal back plate
f Midgut or ventriculus
g Heart
h Ovaries
i Anterior intestine
j Scent gland
k Rectum
l Anus
m Antenna
n Mouth cavity

o Mandibular gland
p Mandibles
q Mouth opening
r Tongue (proboscis)
s Brain (lower ganglion)
t Nerve cord
u Heart spiral (nine
  turns)
v Honey sac or stomach
w and x Proventricular
  valve, a narrow, funnel-
  like passage
y Wax gland
z Sting

Lengthwise vertical section of a bee. The bee's tripartite body (head, thorax, and abdomen) is enclosed by an exoskeleton consisting of chitin. Three pairs of legs and two pairs of wings are attached to the thorax. Bees breathe through tracheal tubes that open through breathing pores in the thorax, called spiracles.

discourage swarming (see page 26). If the beekeeper stands by idly, the queen will soon leave the hive with about a third of the workers (the prime swarm). The bees usually alight on a branch and hang there in a tight cluster with the queen in the middle. If the beekeeper does not catch the swarm at this point (see page 31), the bees will scout out and take off for a new permanent home in a hollow tree, a hole in the ground, or a rock crevice and will then be lost to the beekeeper for good. Almost half of the remaining bees may also move out seven days after the departure of the prime swarm, taking one

or several of the new queens with them (the after-swarm). Only the brood, some young nurse bees, and a few new queens are left in the hive. These latter will fight each other to the death until only one remains. After five days the virgin queen is sexually mature and takes off on her nuptial flight.

Drones that are ready to mate leave their hive in early afternoon usually between 2 and 3 o'clock. They fly around near their hives or gather in drone congregating areas where the weather conditions are favorable and where the drones stay aloft 15–40 feet (5–12 m) above the ground.

The mating always takes place in the air. In the act of copulation, the drone's genitalia, which are normally located inside the tip of the abdomen, are extruded by turning inside out and enter the queen's vagina pouch. The spermatozoa are discharged into the queen's vagina and gradually move from there to a sperm-holding reservoir called the spermatheca. The drone expires in the course of copulation. A queen may mate with five to eight drones during her five to six weeks of sexual receptivity. In the process she accumulates millions of spermatozoa, enough to last a lifetime of egg laying.

Sometimes the workers replace an old queen with a new one without the colony's swarming. The old queen either dies or is killed by a virgin queen or by the workers. This process, which is advantageous for the apiarist because the colony is rejuvenated without any effort on his or her part, is called supersedure.

Once the young queen has mated and started a good brood nest, the drones no longer serve a useful function. They consume food without contributing to the life of the hive, and the worker bees begin to expel them from the hive or kill them.

Worker bees born in August or later winter over and don't die until the next spring. From November on no more brood is raised, and the entire colony collects in a tight cluster around the queen. The bees feed on the honey they have gathered and stored for winter, converting carbohydrates into body heat. The temperature at the center of the cluster stays between 68 and 77°F (20–25°C) and drops to be-

A Short Introduction to Bees

tween 46 and 50°F (8–10°C) on the outside. The stronger a colony is when the winter sets in (10,000–20,000 bees), the easier it is for the bees to maintain the needed temperatures.

In January and February, if the outside temperature in the northern, eastern, and midwestern states rises to 50 or 55°F (10–12°C), the workers take two or three cleansing flights. The winter cluster breaks up temporarily, and the bees fly outside to eliminate their feces. Bees of a healthy, undisturbed colony relieve themselves only outside, never in the hive. The small, yellowish squirts are quite easy to see in the snow.

Most winter bees survive until spring. A few older ones die in the course of the winter and are carried out of the hive on mild days. In February the queen resumes egg laying, and in March the bees start foraging for the first nectar.

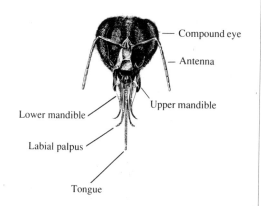

The head of a worker bee. With their large compound eyes bees are able to perceive ultraviolet as well as polarized light. The upper and lower mandibles are used to chew honey and pollen and to knead wax. Bees feel for the nectaries of flowers with their labial palpi, and they have sensory receptors in the antennae that register odors and outside temperature. The tongue, or proboscis, with its taste buds is used to suck the nectar from the nectaries.

Feeding and Pollination

When a worker bee is about 15 days old, she begins to make some orientation flights to become acquainted with the surroundings of the hive. By the time she is 20 days old, she is ready to work as a field bee and starts collecting nectar, honeydew, and pollen whenever the weather is warm enough (60°F, 15°C) and dry.

Nectar is a sweet secretion produced by a flower's glands, which are called nectaries. To get at the nectar, the bee must penetrate deeply into the corolla, where the nectaries usually lie buried. In this process the hairs on her body pick up pollen grains, and since individual bees specialize in particular flowers, visiting only one kind of blossom on any one flight (flower fidelity), they automatically pollinate the flowers with the pollen that clings to them.

The bee absorbs nectar by means of her tongue, or proboscis, and sucks it into her honey sac or stomach, which is connected by a funnel-shaped valve to the digestive tract (see drawing on page 7). The bee absorbs only as much nectar into her digestive system as is needed for her survival.

On the way back to the hive, water begins to be eliminated from the nectar in the honey sac and passed to the intestines. At the same time the nectar is enriched with substances produced by various glands of the bee. When the field bee returns to the hive, she unloads the processed contents of her honey sac into empty cells of the comb by means of her proboscis or passes on the nectar to hive bees, which also process the nectar and then store it in empty cells.

Other hive bees pick up the unripe honey, which is still very thin, process it with enzymes they produce, and then deposit it in other cells. This procedure is repeated over and over until the nectar has turned into honey. Some bees are located between the honeycomb and the hive entrance, beating their wings very fast to move the water that is evaporating from the honey out of the hive (see

A Short Introduction to Bees

photo on page 37). When the water content has been reduced to between 17 and 20%, the honey is ripe, and the bees seal the full honey cells with a thin cover of wax. As soon as this is done, the bee-keeper can start extracting honey (see page 36).

Depending on the productiveness of the plant sources, bees must make about 40,000 trips and visit between three and five million blossoms to harvest 2 pounds (1 kg) of honey. The capacity of a bee's honey stomach is about 50–60 mg.

A bee colony that is located in a forested area can start harvesting honeydew in June. This honeydew is produced by aphids of the Lachnidae family and various scale insects of the Lecanidae family. These insects suck the sap of pine, fir, and spruce needles and sometimes also of the leaf stems of oaks, maples, and other deciduous trees to absorb the nutritional substances they need. The rest of the sap is excreted and hangs in shiny droplets on the needles or leaves of the trees. In Europe a distinction is made between honey that comes from evergreen trees and honey from deciduous trees: The former is called forest honey; the latter, leaf honey. Honeydew, which is processed in the hive just like nectar, has an inferior flavor and is not properly acceptable as honey.

The honey that is deposited in combs is intended for rearing the brood and as food for the cold winter months. The carbohydrates contained in it supply the bees with the energy needed for their activities.

Bees need not only carbohydrates, which they obtain from nectar and honeydew; they also gather pollen, which supplies them with protein. While they fly from flower to flower, they brush the pollen off their hairy coats with the help of brush-like hairs on their legs and pack it into pocketlike indentations, called pollen baskets, in their hind legs (see drawing on page 7). There the pollen is mixed with a bit of honey the bee carried with her from the hive and kneaded into a solid clump. An experienced beekeeper can tell what flowers a bee has visited from the color of the pollen pellets. Back at the hive the bee strips off the pollen into an empty cell, where young hive bees compress it by "stamping" it in place with their forelegs and heads.

Round Dance and Wag-tail Dance

When a bee has found a good source of food within a radius of about 300 feet (100 m) and on level terrain, she can announce this to the bees in the hive by performing what is called a round dance. What she does is to fly around rapidly in a circle,

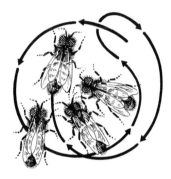

Bees perform the "round dance" to communicate to other field bees that there is a food source within 300 feet (100 m) of the hive.

first to the left, then to the right (see drawing above). Some of the surrounding bees touch the dancing bee and then start dancing, too. With the olfactory organs at the tips of their antennae they have picked up the scent of the flower, which lingers on the field bee's hairy coat. A precise description of the location is unnecessary if it is within 300 feet of the hive, but the abundance of the source is indicated by the speed of the dance. The faster the dance, the richer the source and the closer to the hive. A food source that is farther away requires that more information be communicated. Direction and exact distance are expressed by means of the "wag-tail dance." Here the bee dances straight ahead on the honeycomb while wagging the tail end of her rump back and

A Short Introduction to Bees

The "wag-tail dance" is used to convey information about a food source that is located more than 300 feet (100 m) from the hive.

forth. Then she circles back—without tail wagging—to the beginning of the straight line, dances along it again, and then circles back, turning the other way this time (see drawing above). The number of times the rump is wagged on the straight line within a given time period indicates the distance between the hive and the food source. The slower the wagging, the farther away is the food source.

The sun is used by the bees as a reference point in conveying the direction in which the food is to be found. The angle formed by the line from the hive to the sun and the line from the hive to the food source is the same as the angle between a vertical line and the straight line of the dance (see drawing below). If the straight line of the dance points straight up, this means that food is to be found by flying directly in the direction of the sun.

As the position of the sun moves, so does the angle of the dance. If the sky is overcast, a small break in the clouds is enough for the bees to determine the position of the sun because they are able to detect the vibrations of polarized light in the patch of blue. Even when the cloud cover is unbroken (as long as it is not too thick), bees are able to sense the position of the sun because they sense ultraviolet light.

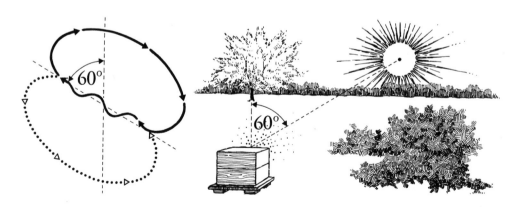

The wag-tail dance also conveys in which direction the food source is to be found. The angle formed by the line from the hive to the sun and the line from the hive to the food source corresponds to the angle formed by a vertical axis and the direction of the straight middle line of the wag-tail dance (the dance is performed on the surface of the combs, which hang down vertically).

A Short Introduction to Bees

How Bees Defend Themselves

There are always some hive bees stationed at the entrance as guards, and almost every bee that approaches is sniffed. If the guards recognize the characteristic odor of the hive, the bee is allowed to enter. A field bee from another colony that is carrying nectar or honey is allowed to pass too. Bees not carrying food may be potential robbers, however, and are driven away.

Bees hardly ever get lost trying to find their way home to the hive because in good flying weather there are not only guard bees stationed at the entry but also other workers that fan the hive scent toward the returning foragers by beating their wings fast with the rump raised high. This helps the field bees recognize their particular hive.

If wasps or hornets approach the hive entrance, their evil intentions are obvious. These insects are not only carnivorous but they also like to eat honey. Their appearance triggers instant attack. Additional hive bees quickly come to the aid of the guards. In such a battle the bees sometimes resort to their venomous stings, which they can extract again after use from the unelastic chitin shell of a wasp or hornet. If a bee stings a human or some other mammal, however, the elastic tissue of the stung victim contracts around the wound, and the barbs of the sting become embedded. When the bee flies off, she leaves the sting behind and with it usually the stinging mechanism and nerve strands. Having lost these parts of her anatomy, she dies.

If the sting with its poison sac is not removed instantly (see page 14), the venom is automatically pumped through the sting into the wound.

Development and Tasks of a Worker Bee

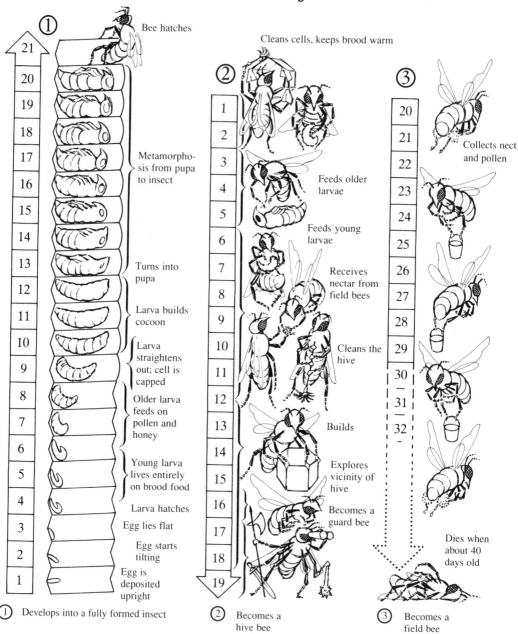

Bee hatches

Cleans cells, keeps brood warm

① 21 20 19 18 17 16 15 14 13 12 11 10 9 8 7 6 5 4 3 2 1

Metamorphosis from pupa to insect

Turns into pupa

Larva builds cocoon

Larva straightens out; cell is capped

Older larva feeds on pollen and honey

Young larva lives entirely on brood food

Larva hatches

Egg lies flat

Egg starts tilting

Egg is deposited upright

② 1 2 3 4 5 6 7 8 9 10 11 12 13 14 15 16 17 18 19

Feeds older larvae

Feeds young larvae

Receives nectar from field bees

Cleans the hive

Builds

Explores vicinity of hive

Becomes a guard bee

③ 20 21 22 23 24 25 26 27 28 29 30 31 32

Collects nect and pollen

Dies when about 40 days old

① Develops into a fully formed insect

② Becomes a hive bee

③ Becomes a field bee

Conditions for Keeping Bees

The Right Location for Your Bees

Where will you put your bees? This is a question you must settle before you embark on beekeeping. The hives should be away from human dwellings. A place near an orchard, the edge of woods, or some unused land is ideal—somewhere where the colonies are undisturbed and have access to good forage within a radius of 1 or 2 miles (1.6–3.2 km) and where you can perform the necessary chores undisturbed. If you plan to keep bees in your garden (which should be at least about an acre), the hives must be placed at some distance from a neighbor's land. A visual barrier about 6 feet (2 m) high made up of bamboo mats or, better yet, a hedge of tall bushes or other plants will keep the bees from being a nuisance to your neighbors. If your garden includes fruit trees and thus offers a ready source of food for your bees, this is of course a great advantage. Setting up a small pond to satisfy the bee's need for water is also a good idea. Most states require registration and have laws regulating honeybees and beekeeping. For more details, please contact the U.S. Department of Agriculture and your county extension services, which publish pamphlets on various aspects of beekeeping.

A colony of bees uses up about 120 pounds (50 kg) of nectar or honeydew and about 45 pounds (20 kg) of pollen from March through September for its own needs (see page 8). The plants that provide this food are sometimes called forage or honey plants. You can assist your bees' labors and enhance the strength of the colonies by sowing nectar-producing plants in your own garden or on land nearby that is not being used for anything else. (Discuss the idea first with the owner of the land and get whatever permission may be necessary from local authorities.) When you pick the spot for your hives, try to find an experienced beekeeper to advise you. You will also want this person's advice if you decide to plant a forage crop for your bees.

Practical Training

Before you acquire bees you should spend a season helping an established beekeeper look after his or her colonies. Sometimes weekend courses are offered by state agricultural colleges or by beekeepers' organizations, in which you can get some firsthand experience working with bees. For more theoretical learning you can turn to a number of textbooks. If your ambition is simply to keep some bees in your backyard and perhaps make a little money from selling honey—which is the case for the majority of beekeepers—you will not need any further training. A professional beekeeper, however, must go through more extensive preparations. In Germany an apprenticeship of 3 years plus 5–10 years of experience as an apiarist are required before an individual is allowed to operate a professional beekeeping operation. To become a professional apiarist you must also be willing to accept some risk and not be afraid of hard physical work.

Bee Stings and Allergies

Bee breeders in our day are particularly intent on producing nonaggressive strains, of which the Americanized Italian bee, the carniolan bee, and the caucasian bee are the most popular. Carniolan bees, which are the race I mainly work with and which I recommend to any beginner, are exceptionally gentle. Still, bee stings cannot be avoided altogether. Since bees sting only when they feel threatened, however, you can modify your behavior to minimize the chances of being stung. Whenever you work with bees, you should avoid abrupt or hectic movement. You should also make sure you're not wearing perfume or using toiletries that are perfumed because these scents arouse the bees. Wearing appropriate clothing (see page 22) also helps protect against bee stings.

Conditions for Keeping Bees

If you are stung, it is important to remove the sting with its poison sac quickly so that as little of the venom as possible enters the body. Don't try to grasp the sting with your fingers and pull it out. This only causes the poison sac to empty out the rest of the venom into the wound. Instead, either brush the sting off with your fingernail without compressing it, or get hold of it between the poison sac and your skin with pincers and pull it out.

The swelling caused by bee stings can be alleviated by applying a compress of rubbing alcohol, saltwater, or onion juice, or with a commercial medicine, of which there are many.

If an individual is stung inside the mouth or in the throat or responds to being stung with dizziness or vomiting, or if an individual collapses after a massive attack of bees, call a doctor immediately.

First aid for swelling inside the mouth or throat—this could lead to suffocation: Sprinkle table salt all over the oral cavity by the spoonful (make sure none of the salt is swallowed!); spit out, and repeat several times. Get the victim to a doctor as quickly as possible.

If you know you are allergic but are not sure whether the allergy is triggered by exposure to bees or only in response to being stung, there are tests allergists can give you to find out the answer. There are effective countermeasures for allergies to bee venom, so the fact that you are allergic doesn't necessarily mean that you have to give up the idea of beekeeping. (For more information, write to the Office of Apiculture, Department of Entomology, Cornell University, Ithaca, New York 14850.)

Costs and Time Commitment

It is difficult to give a specific answer to the question of costs. Beekeeping is affected by weather and the health of the colonies, and the annual outlay for food and the prevention or treatment of disease is hard to predict accurately—and so is the likely income you may expect from the sale of honey and other beekeeping products.

You must figure on initial costs for three hives (hive bodies, supers, accessories, clothes, and other equipment) amounting to approximately $500. The price of bees for two colonies is about $200. Add to this annually about $10 for disease control, $60 for food for the bees, $40 for dues, and about $50 for literature. This means that if you start with new equipment you will invest between $800 and $900 the first year.

You don't need to buy expensive harvesting equipment, such as an extractor (see page 36), to start with. Chances are that an apiarist in your area will let you borrow this equipment or you may be able to buy one cooperatively with another beekeeper.

If you take over bees and equipment from a beekeeper who wants to give up bees, your costs will of course be much less. You will probably be able to get 10 colonies with all the necessary equipment for about $2000. Beekeepers' magazines often have ads for bees and equipment for sale by retiring apiarists. Before you commit yourself to buying, however, ask the advice of an experienced beekeeper.

Beginners and people wanting to keep bees as a hobby will not count the hours they spend with the bees as work. Apiarists with several years of experience figure they put in six to eight hours a year per colony. This includes only the time spent actually working with the bees, not the job of keeping the equipment in good shape and repairing it.

Apiary Organizations

I urge you strongly to join a beekeepers' organization. Membership not only provides you with advice on legal and insurance questions but also entitles you to take advantage at lower rates of many services offered by local and state groups.

There are state beekeeping organizations in every state, many local beekeepers' associations,

Conditions for Keeping Bees

and regional organizations. You may find out more about these groups by contacting other local beekeepers, your county agricultural extension service, or your state department of agriculture.

The state organizations foster cooperation between scientists and practicing beekeepers. In their publications they inform beekeepers of research that is being done on bees and beekeeping at state universities. Many states have beekeeping specialists who assist beekeepers with advice and information. State organizations also have the addresses of apiaries where courses for beginners as well as advanced beekeepers are offered. (See also Bibliography and Useful Addresses, page 66.)

In the European countries that belong to the Common Market, the interests of beekeepers are represented by COPA, an agency with headquarters in Brussels that heads all groups involved in agricultural production. There is also an international association of beekeepers with worldwide membership, called Apimondia, with offices in Bucharest, Romania, and Rome, Italy. According to information from Apimondia there are about 1.4 million beekeepers worldwide with approximately 12 million colonies of bees.

Insurance and Taxes

In many states, members of a local beekeepers' association can get insurance for losses of colonies, equipment, and stores of food for the bees. You can also insure your full honey harvest against damage during transport, through fire, theft, vandalism (the willful harming of bees by others), storms, flooding, and damage from the use of pesticides and herbicides. In addition, you, the members of your family, and any employees engaged in the beekeeping operation can get insurance against accidents, disability, or death as a result of beekeeping operations. In case of litigation connected with beekeeping, you may be able to apply for reimbursement of costs for legal services and for expert opinions. Clarify in advance which of these costs are covered. Your local or state organization can also supply you with a list of benefits and any ordinances applying to beekeeping.

For tax purposes, beekeeping is considered an agricultural occupation. Therefore, if you are a hobbyist, this means that you are required to pay taxes on money you received for honey and other bee products you sold.

Bee Hives, Equipment, and Colonies

What Kind of Hives Are Practical?

The two types of hives most commonly used are movable-frame, such as the Langstroth hives and the William Broughton Carr or WBC hives, top-opening hives, and the so-called leaf hives that are worked from behind. Leaf hives must be kept in a bee house, whereas movable-frame hives can be set up outdoors or in a bee house. Since not many beginning beekeepers are likely to buy or build a house and will therefore probably keep their bees in movable-frame hives, I will in the following chapters first describe each work procedure as it applies to a movable-frame hive.

There are a few other methods of housing bees that I mention briefly on page 20.

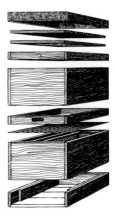

A movable-frame hive is worked from above. It consists of (from bottom to top): a bottom board; a hive body (brood chamber) with room for eight to ten hanging frames; a queen excluder (to keep the queen out of the honey chamber); a separator board; an upper hive body or super (honey chamber); a feeding cover with feeder trough; a grate that allows air exchange during transport; an insulating cover; an outer cover.

Movable-frame Hives

A movable-frame hive (sometimes called the Langstroth hive, after L. L. Langstroth, a great nineteenth century pioneer of modern beekeeping and of this type of hive design) consists of a rectangular bottom board with a rim 1–4 inches (3–10 cm) high, onto which two or more wooden boxes without tops or bottoms, called hive bodies, are set. (The hive body on the bottom is called the brood chamber, and the ones on top, used by the bees for honey storage, are generally referred to as supers.) On top of the hive bodies is a cover and, perhaps, an inner lid of insulating material for colder weather or a ventilation screen (a layer of wire mesh fitted into a narrow wooden frame) that is inserted for transporting the bees. All the parts—from the bottom board to the lid—have the same rectangular dimensions so that they can be stacked neatly. The hive entrance, a small rectangular opening, is located on the front of the hive in the rim of the bottom board. With this type of hive the frames for the honeycombs are hung into and taken out of the hive bodies from the top, which means that the work with the colonies is done from the top.

As protection against moisture from underneath, the hives should be set up a foot or a foot and a half off the ground on hive stands or a stack of beams or wooden boards. The top of a hive standing by itself should be protected against the weather with a protruding outer cover of waterproof material; several hives set up in a row can be covered with a roof of wood, metal, or roofing paper.

It is possible to set up movable-frame hives in a bee house (see page 21), but it is easier to work this type of hive outdoors.

Exchange of ideas and experience is an important prerequisite for successful beekeeping. When you handle bees, appropriate, bee-proof clothing is essential.

Bee Hives, Equipment, and Colonies

Advantages of Movable-frame Hives

• There is no need for a bee house.
• The hive space can be adjusted to the size of the colony by adding supers as needed. An easy way to form nucleus colonies is to add supers with queen excluders (see page 34).
• There is no need for special nucleus boxes (small hives).
• In the winter you can use the empty hive bodies for storing empty combs. Use separator boards as tops and bottoms for stacked hive bodies to keep out mice. This means that you don't need to buy or build special, rodent-proof cabinets for the combs.
• The frames filled with honey can be transported to an extractor inside the hive bodies, thus eliminating the need for special transport boxes.
• You will have a greater honey harvest than with leaf hives because the colonies are stronger.

The Disadvantages of Movable-frame Hives

Movable-frame hives require more physical strength than leaf-hives because sometimes hive bodies full of combs must be lifted. A super with all the frames filled with honey can weigh close to 50 pounds (20 kg).

Leaf Hives

A leaf hive (see drawing on page 20) consists of a wooden box that is subdivided by a horizontal metal grid into two equal spaces, the brood chamber below and the honey chamber above. The spaces of

Above: A comb with sealed worker brood. The brood nest is solidly filled and extends over the entire comb. In the two upper corners, honey and pollen are stored.
Below, left: Bees are being brushed off a comb with a bee brush. Right: A comb occupied by bees (left in photo) has been removed from the brood chamber and is about to be replaced with fresh foundation.

this excluder grid are large enough for the worker bees to pass through but too small for the queen. This way only worker bees can get at the combs in the upper chamber to deposit honey there. The combs containing the brood (the brood nest) are all in the chamber below. Since only combs from the top are taken out for honey extraction (see page 36), there is no chance of larvae being in the combs meant for honey production.

An inch or so above the bottom of the leaf hive and above the built-in excluder grid are racks of horizontal metal bars. The frames for the combs are slid onto these bars so that they are lined up vertically on the bars of the rack. When one frame is removed, the others can be moved to the right or left as needed. A leaf hive is worked from behind because the frames are taken out and inserted from the side opposite the hive entrance. The back wall of the brood chamber is made up of a wooden frame with a glass window. On the inside of this window frame there is an empty wooden frame that the bees can fill with combs. This is called the building frame. The type of cells constructed by the bees in this frame—worker, drone, or queen cells—indicates the mood of the colony (see page 25). (In a movable-frame hive an empty frame hung next to the brood nest fulfills the same function of "mood-indicator.") On the back wall of the honey chamber there is a wooden frame with a glass window or wire screen. The entire back side of the leaf hive is closed off by a wooden door. Most leaf hives come with pads that help insulate the brood and honey chambers.

Advantages of a Leaf Hive

• Leaf hives can be stacked one on top of the other.
• If leaf hives are located in a row at the right height, work with the bees can be done sitting down, a feature that is especially advantageous for older or physically handicapped persons.
• The glass window makes it possible to watch the bees without disturbing them, and the building frame that serves as mood indicator of the colony is open to view.

19

Bee Hives, Equipment, and Colonies

Disadvantages of a Leaf Hive

• Leaf hives must be housed in a building.

• A fitted tray (a wooden board with rims 2–5 inches, 5–10 cm, high on three sides) is needed. It is hung on the back of the hive. Bees that are brushed off a frame that is taken out of the hive (see page 29) drop onto this tray and can return easily to the hive.

• The frames that are taken out of the hive are placed in a frame rack with slots for 8–10 frames. The slots are spaced so that the bees are not squashed between the frames when you set down the frames.

• You must have a special storage cabinet for frames that are not in use during winter. The storage cabinet should have built-in racks into which the frames fit individually.

• To work comfortably behind the hives in the bee house, you should have a small worktable where your tools are handy and you can deposit the filled frames in the frame rack. If you have two or three hives on top of each other, you should have a table that can be raised or lowered so that it is always at a convenient level for the hive you happen to be working with.

Other Types of Hives

A *trough hive* is worked from above and must be protected against the weather. Consequently it must be set up in either a bee house or a small outdoor shelter (see page 21).

Original *Zander hives* are still used quite extensively in Germany and many other parts of Europe. These hives are a precursor of the modern movable-frame hive but are not suitable for an outdoor apiary.

Before the introduction of modern hives, beekeepers used inverted baskets of wicker or straw, called *skeps*. Skeps are still used in parts of Europe and the United States today, but their primary function is decorative.

Another ancient method of housing bees is the "bee gum" or log hive. This is, of course, the kind of housing wild bees choose. A bee gum consists of a

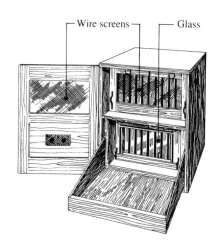

Wire screens — Glass

A leaf hive is worked from behind, and this drawing shows the rear of the hive. The hive is made up of a brood chamber (below) and a honey chamber (above). The queen excluder is built in. A ventilation window in the upper half of the door and a wooden frame that closes off the honey room are both filled with wire screening. A building frame is mounted on the frame of the brood chamber window. The brood chamber window is also equipped with a thin board that can be inserted in the window during transport or when the bees are brushed off the combs. The attachable tray is used only when the back door of the hive is open.

hollow log with crossed sticks at the top to support honeycombs. The top is then covered with a board, and a hole in the bottom serves as the entrance.

Necessary Equipment

Bee journals and specialized catalogs advertise hives and all the standard equipment. You can also get parts for the different types of hives, which will be sent to you with instructions on how to assemble them. In the literature on beekeeping (see page 66),

Bee Hives, Equipment, and Colonies

you will find addresses of mail-order houses. You can write for free catalogs and price lists. In some areas, beekeepers form associations that enable them to get cheaper wholesale prices and to market their honey cooperatively.

I recommend that a beginning beekeeper start out with two colonies. More than this is hard to manage at first, and if you have only one, you have no basis for comparison. If that one colony dies, you must start from scratch again.

For two colonies you will need:
• 3 hives (one is needed for starting new colonies; see pages 26 and 30)
• Frames (for sizes, see page 24) with drawn comb: about 20 per hive
• Foundations: about 8–12 per colony
• A roll of reinforcement wire (8 ounces)
• Feeders for three hives
• 3 record cards
• 1 pollen feeder
• 1 solar wax melter
• 2–3 queen or hatching cages for queen cells
• 1 box for an artificial swarm
• 1 mating box
• 1 queen-marking set
• 1 bee smoker with tobacco or other suitable fuel (see page 65)
• 1 water sprayer
• 1 each: hive tool, brush, scraper, spur embedder
• If you keep bees in leaf hives, you will also need a bee house, a frame rack, a comb storage cabinet, and a nucleus box.

In the chapter on care and management (page 24) you will find instructions on when and how to use the various tools and other items of equipment.

What You Can Build Yourself

The initial costs can be reduced considerably if you build some of the equipment yourself.

To protect your hives from the weather you can build an outdoor shelter consisting of three walls

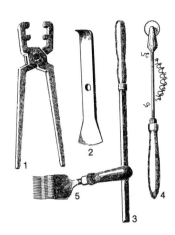

These are the tools an amateur beekeeper needs:
1 Tongs to move frames in a leaf hive. **2** Hive tool for loosening combs. **3** Honey stirrer, which is a three-sided wooden (beech) stick. **4** Spur-wheel embedder for mounting foundation in frame. **5** Uncapping fork with bent tines used for lifting wax caps off honeycombs.

and a roof. A structure that is about 8 feet (250 cm) long, 2 feet (60 cm) deep and 5 feet (150 cm) tall and rests on a stand about 8–12 inches (20–30 cm) high can accommodate five hives. The roof must be made of roofing felt or some other waterproof material.

A useful feature is to have a hinged back wall that can be flipped up to protect the beekeeper against rain and sun while he or she is working with the hives. This way the bees can go about their business without interfering in your work.

A bee house for bees kept in leaf hives can also be built at home. If you decide to build such a structure, make it large enough to include a separate work and honey extraction room, which must be absolutely bee proof, however. There should also be room in the bee house for storing the various beekeeping tools and other accessories that you will need.

Bee Hives, Equipment, and Colonies

If you are clever with tools you can also build a pollen feeder (similar to a small birdhouse) and the worktable for a leaf hive (see drawing on page 20) yourself.

Clothing

Overalls made of a light, white material have proven useful protective clothing for working with bees. To keep the bees from crawling inside the clothes, the suit is equipped with a zipper in front, and the cuffs of the sleeves and pants have elastic bands in the seams. Don't wear dark or woolen clothes; dark colors and wool seem to irritate bees.

To protect your face, head, and hands from being stung wear light-colored gloves and a beekeeper's hat with a veil. Once you feel more comfortable handling bees you can dispense with the gloves, but there is no need to test your courage as a beginner.

Choosing the Right Race

For a beginner I recommend starting out with the Italian bee, *Apis mellifera linguistica*, America's most popular race, or, my favorite, the carniolan or Austrian bees, *Apis mellifera carnica* (see photo on page 55). The latter, which are characterized by gray bands on the abdomen but are very similar to the Italian bee, offer a number of advantages:
• They are so gentle that you will be able to work with them soon without wearing gloves.
• They remain on the combs without becoming excited when you work with the hive. This is a particularly useful trait when you are looking for the queen. More excitable bees may retreat to the hive walls or some dark corner as soon as you remove a comb.
• Carniolan bees develop brood quickly, and the colonies therefore grow rapidly.
• Through selective breeding, this race can be adapted well to existing conditions, such as the size of the hives and the location.

The Right Time to Get Started

The best time to buy bees or take over colonies in their hives is the spring. With this timing you will be able to harvest some honey the first year. Colonies with or without queens (see pages 30 and 34) and swarms (see page 7), that is, bees without hives, can be bought in June or July. If you attend beekeepers' meetings, you can ask around about who is selling new or established colonies, or you can consult beekeepers' magazines.

Transporting the Bees

It doesn't matter whether a novice starts with an established colony, a colony without a queen, or a swarm. There are a few rules that must be observed, however, both in transporting bees and in getting them established in their new location. The best time to move bees is evening. Hives with bees in them must never be left in the full sun. It is essential that the bees get enough oxygen because they panic if the oxygen gets low. In their agitation they use up more oxygen, which in turn excites them more, and gradually the temperature in the hive begins to rise. If it reaches 140°F (60°C), the wax begins to melt, the combs collapse, and the colony perishes.

So if you plan to move a colony in its hive, make sure to replace the inner insulating lid with a ventilation grid (see drawing on page 16). An even better way is to use hives with transport floors, that is, bottom boards with rims about 5 inches (10 cm) high and with fine wire screening on two opposite sides. During travel, the bees can leave their combs and hang in clusters from the bottom bars of the frames, where they get plenty of fresh air through the screening.

Bee Hives, Equipment, and Colonies

The frames inside the hive body should be held together securely with a belt for the trip. The belt is removed when the hive is set up in its new location.

If you transport bees in leaf hives, remove the heating pads and secure the windows of the brood chamber and the honey chamber with small nails or with window locks mounted on the window frame. In many leaf hives, the door at the back has a screen panel that can be covered with a wooden flap (see drawing on page 20). Open this flap for the trip. You should also push up the small wooden board that is attached to the window of the brood chamber so that the bees can escape through a slot into the space between the window and the door, where they can hang in a cluster.

If you buy a colony or a nucleus minus the hive, the bees come on combs that must be—and this is an important point—on frames that fit your hive. If the combs are not the right size for your hive body, they must be trimmed to fit.

A swarm is transported in a swarm catcher, which is simply an oblong box with fine screening on at least two sides so that the bees get plenty of air.

Setting Up a Colony

Colonies and nuclei in hives are set up immediately after they arrive in the location intended for them. The entrances are opened and the screen sections of the bottom boards closed off with solid sections. If you use a leaf hive, the heating pad is turned on once the bees have settled on the combs again.

If you have caught a swarm, let it rest for an hour or two in the swarm catcher in a cool, shady place (a cellar, for instance) before transferring it to the hive. This is best done in the evening. On the cover of the swarm catcher there is usually a piece of burlap from which a cluster of bees will be hanging. Pick up the cover with the cluster, hold it over the open hive or the tray of a leaf hive, and give it a good whack or two. The bees will drop into the hive or onto the tray and immediately move onto the combs. Then you take the swarm-catching box, which still contains bees, turn it upside down over the hive and give it a whack too so that the remaining bees will join the rest of the swarm.

Care and Management

In this chapter I explain all the chores a bee-keeper must perform in order to harvest as much honey as possible. A chronological listing of what needs to be done month by month is given under the heading The Beekeeper's Yearly Work Cycle (see page 46).

Assembling the Frames

To add stability to the combs that the bees build, the foundation in the frames has wires embedded in it. In the United States and England, unfortunately, many different sizes of frames are in use. I recommend to the beginner the most common frame, the Hoffman or self-spacing frame. With this type it is impossible to make the mistake of putting too many or two few frames in each hive. The frames are spaced by the extra thickness of wood at the top of the side bars. This spacing, often called the Hoffman spacing, is usually $1\frac{1}{2}$ or $1\frac{3}{8}$ inches (3.8 or 3.5 cm) center to center.

If you want to build your own frames, you should make sure to get the standard thickness of wood from a supplier of bee equipment. The ends of the frame bars are coated with a water-insoluble glue before they are nailed together at a 90° angle at the corners.

Wiring the Frames

The foundation is a sheet of wax the size of the inside dimensions of the frame. To attach it securely to the frame, the frame must be reinforced or "wired" (see drawing in next column). Use a hand or electric drill or a special beekeeper's awl (available from beekeepers' suppliers) to drill four or six small holes (depending on the make of the equipment you are using) along the centerline of the two bars that make up the longer sides of the frame. The outer holes are drilled about 1 inch (3 cm) from the ends; the remaining two or four holes are spaced so that all holes are at an equal distance from each

other. Then take two small nails or tacks and tap them into the ends of one bar between the outer holes and the ends. Don't tap them in all the way but leave enough room to be able to wind the reinforcing wire around them.

Now you are ready to thread the wire through the hole next to one tack, then through the corresponding hole on the opposite bar, then through the next hole on the same bar, back to the slat you started on, and so on, as though you were stitching the bars together. You will finish at the hole next to the second tack. Wrap the end of the wire around this tack; then start pulling on the loose end until the wire between the tacks is tight but doesn't bend the bars. Wrap this end around the tack next to it, and nail the tacks in all the way.

Wiring a frame. Tighten the threaded wire with pliers, and secure the ends of wire by wrapping them around a tack that is hammered into the wooden frame. The frame is now ready for the foundation, which can be embedded with a spur-wheel embedder or a transformer.

Fastening the Foundation

To fasten the foundation to the frame, you need a small wooden board a hair smaller than the frame's inside dimensions and half the thickness of the frame. (If the frame's depth is $\frac{1}{2}$ inch (10–12 cm), the board would have to be just barely $\frac{1}{4}$ inch (5–6 cm) thick. The wire can be embedded in the foundation either with a hand embedding tool (spur embedder) or with a small electric transformer.

24

Care and Management

• A spur embedder is a small, movable cogwheel with grooved teeth (see drawing on page 21). Lay a sheet of foundation on the small wooden board, and then place a wired frame on top of the foundation. Heat the embedding tool over a small flame, and then run it along the wire in the frame. The heat of the tool warms the wire, which melts the wax of the foundation and becomes embedded in it.

• If you have more than ten colonies, it makes sense to invest in a small electric transformer (about $50). With this device you can use low-voltage electricity to fasten the foundation. For this procedure you place the wired frame on the wooden board and the foundation on top of the frame. Then, touch the two ends of the electric cable to the heads of the tacks so that the electric circuit is closed. The wire and the wax on top of it are warmed by the current, and the foundation's own weight causes it to combine with the wire. When the wire cools, frame and foundation are securely connected. The entire process takes no more than a few seconds.

Insulating Hives and Spring Feeding

During spells of cold weather it is especially hard for the bees to maintain an even brood temperature of 95°F (35°C). Think of it this way: The more heat the bees must generate themselves, the shorter their life span. This is why you should wrap the hives with thick cloth and cover them with a tarpaulin. You should also angle a board 4–8 inches (10–20 cm) wide from the entrance to the ground. This ramp makes it easier for the bees to make their way back into the hive when it rains.

When it is cold and rainy, bees cannot go out foraging. Thus it can happen that there is not enough food for the brood. To prevent this most dire situation, observe the following rule of thumb: In the spring, there should be at least four or five filled combs in the outer frames of every hive, the combs partially occupied by bees, and about two-thirds of the cells capped. This is the equivalent of approximately 20–25 pounds (10–12 kg) of food. If there are fewer-filled combs, you can take out empty combs close to the brood nest and replace them with filled ones that you remove from a colony that has a plentiful store of food.

You can also give the bees a boost by feeding them Candy for Bees, Hard Candy for Winter (or "sugar boards," as thin slabs of this prepared material are usually called), or sugar syrup. Once you have established how much food the bees need, you give them the appropriate amount (for amounts and feeders, see pages 40–42).

Feeding bees in the spring also has another purpose, namely, to stimulate brood rearing. For this purpose, however, bee candy or sugar syrup alone is not enough. The bees also need pollen. This is why you should offer your bees a pollen substitute (brewer's yeast or soy flour) in the spring in a pollen feeder ("birdhouse" feeder). Set up the pollen feeder in a sunny spot near the hives, making sure that the distance between the feeding surface and the roof of the feeder is at least 8–10 inches (20–25 cm). The bees need room to hover while they are packing the food into their pollen baskets (see page 8).

It is important not to start a feeding intended to stimulate brood rearing too early. Wait until after the gooseberry bushes flower. Otherwise the bees build too large a brood nest and will not be able to maintain the necessary temperature during cold weather. If the brood nest becomes too cool, the brood dies, and the overworked bees become susceptible to sickness and may die prematurely.

Cutting Out the Building Frame

A strong colony begins to occupy the building frame in April (see page 47). Some building bees attach themselves to the upper frame bar and form a cluster there. These bees proceed to "sweat" the wax (see page 5), with which they build combs. They usually start in several spots all at once, building heart-shaped sections of comb that are later connected into one seamless comb. While the days lengthen (see drawing on page 44), that is, until the summer solstice, bees build primarily drone cells, since drones must be raised in time for a virgin queen's nuptial flight in June or July (see page 7). When the building activity in the building frame lets up and the worker bees start shaping queen cells, the bees may be getting ready to swarm. The building frame thus serves as a kind of mood indicator of the colony. Every time the frame has filled, you should cut out the comb (run a sharp knife along the inside of the frame) so that the bees can start building combs again and you can again assess their mood.

Place combs you have cut out in the garden for a few days. Birds like to pick the grubs out of them. The wax can be melted in a solar wax heater (see drawing on page 41) and bartered in exchange for foundation, or you can keep the wax yourself and perhaps make beeswax candles out of it in the winter.

Methods to Prevent Swarming

Since bees intent on swarming (usually as early as March in the Southern states, and in July in the far north) lose interest in collecting nectar and raising brood and some of the honey harvest is lost if a colony swarms, you will want to try to suppress the swarming impulse or prevent the bees from taking off. The measures that need to be taken for this purpose are some of the most important activities of a beekeeper interested in obtaining maximum honey production.

Colony Expansion

As soon as a colony has filled all the cells in the brood chamber and if there is still room in the hive body, the bees must be given more space. To ac-complish this, hang a frame with foundation (see page 24) or an empty comb next to the brood nest. From June on you can also hang these expansion frames directly into the brood nest. Keep adding frames until the brood chamber is full. When you add foundation, you should each time move the combs with the oldest brood to the outer edge of the brood nest. Then, when the brood has hatched, the combs can be filled with honey and, at the end of the honey season, they can be cut out (see disease prevention, page 57).

Opening up the Honey Chamber or Adding Supers

In May—in warmer regions as early as April—you should examine each colony carefully and check to see how healthy it is, whether the brood nest is well filled, and if there are any signs of disease (see page 57). In a normally developed colony, a good three-fourths of the combs are filled with brood by early May (or earlier in warmer climates), with the bees hanging below the combs in a cluster. This is the time to open up the honey chamber.

If you are working with a movable-frame hive, the following items should be ready: an empty super, a queen excluder (see drawing on page 16), a queen cage (a small cage made of wood or synthetic material; see drawings on pages 31 and 32), a queen-catching glass (see drawing on page 32), one or two frames with foundation (see page 24), and eight or nine frames with empty combs.

Above: An apiary with leaf hives. The small nucleus boxes (on the right, next to the regular hives) are used for rearing queens.
Below: A temporary hive stand that can be disassembled for transport. The entrances to the hives are marked in different colors to help returning bees find their own colony.

Care and Management

If you have a leaf hive, you will need one or two frames with foundation and eight or nine with empty combs, a queen cage, and a queen-catching glass.

While you actually work in the hive, you should blow a little smoke into it now and then to calm the bees (see page 64).

The steps described in the following paragraphs are the same for both a movable-frame hive and a leaf hive.

To make sure that the queen does not get lost or hurt in the process of shifting frames, she should temporarily be isolated for her own protection. Search systematically through the combs to find her. When you have spotted her, invert the bulging end of the queen-catching glass over her. She will then start crawling up the glass tube. Remove the plug from the queen cage, set the bulging end of the queen catcher over the opening, and blow the queen into the cage, which you then close again with the plug. Experienced beekeepers remove the queen by hand, grasping her wings carefully with two fingers and guiding her into the cage.

Attach the queen cage with some wire to a brood comb from the brood chamber so that it is clearly visible, and return the comb to the brood chamber. Then move two or three other brood combs from the brood chamber into the super (in a movable-frame hive) or into the honey chamber (in a leaf hive).

If you fail to locate the queen, you must brush the bees off the combs that will be moved into the super or the honey chamber. Use a soft broom or a large goose feather, and hold the comb over the brood chamber of a movable-frame hive or the tray of a leaf hive.

Above, left: Removing honeycombs from a movable-comb hive. To calm the bees, a puff of smoke is aimed at them. Right: Lifting the wax covers off the honey cells with an uncapping fork.
Below, left: An extractor with the top opened. Right: The honey flows from the extractor's cock through a double strainer into the honey bucket.

Add one or two frames with foundation and a frame of empty comb next to the combs in the brood chamber. When the brood chamber is again filled with frames, you can release the queen into it. Then lay the queen excluder on top of the hive body housing the brood chamber and put the super with seven or eight frames of empty comb on top of the excluder. This super is now ready to be filled with honey.

If you have a leaf hive, set the empty combs you have gotten ready into the honey chamber, reinstall the windows of the honey chamber and of the brood chamber (the latter with the building frame), and replace the heating pad. Since they now have plenty of space for storing honey again, the bees can go on with their work and the danger of swarming is, for the time being, averted.

Shrinking the Colony

A colony's population increases rapidly in the summer, with 1000–2000 new bees hatching every day. Since congestion is a major factor in swarming, you must take steps to prevent overcrowding. When you examine your colonies, remove one or two sealed brood combs with the bees on them (but without the queen) and replace them with empty combs or with foundation. The brood combs can be added to a weaker but healthy colony, or you can use them to form nuclei (see page 34).

This way you relieve the colony of about 5000-10,000 bees and give the remaining workers enough space to keep brooding activities going. You can repeat this procedure after one or two weeks, but don't remove bees more than three times. This method is about 80% effective in preventing swarming. It only works, however, if it is applied before the bees have started nursing brood in queen cells; that is, before the larvae are being lavishly fed with royal jelly.

As soon as you discover queen cells either in the building frame of a leaf hive or along the edges of the combs in movable-frame hives, you must take swarm-preventive steps by relocating the colony (see below), setting up a nucleus with a queen (see next column), starting an artificial swarm (see page 33), or starting a brood nucleus (see page 34).

Relocating the Colony

If you have stacked leaf hives, this method is more difficult to implement than with hives either of the movable-frame or the leaf type that are placed next to each other. The reason is that all the brood combs of the colony that are ready to swarm must be moved to another hive. The following description is based on a system in which hives are located next to rather than on top of each other.

Move the hive with the restless bees to a spot that is at least 3 feet (1 m) away from its original location. Then take a hive without bees and put it in the vacated spot. This hive is filled with frames with foundation and empty combs (in a leaf hive only the brood chamber is filled) but with enough room left empty in the center for one comb. Now take the brood comb on which the queen sits from the colony you have moved and hang it into the center of the new hive, with all the bees and the queen attached to it. Then you empty about half the remaining bees from the old brood chamber into the new hive.

During the rest of the day, the returning field bees will join the new colony. This new colony—which is really the swarm of the old colony—will deliver just as much honey as a normal colony. The queen cells in the old colony can be used—except for two—for rearing queens (see page 31). If you don't wish to rear queens, the cells should be broken out of the comb and destroyed. When the two remaining queens hatch, the stronger one will kill the weaker one and then proceed to mate (see page 6). The old colony will recover quickly from the loss of some of its workers and its old queen because new bees keep hatching from the remaining brood combs and the queen soon starts to lay new eggs.

A Nucleus with a Queen

Another way to forestall swarming when larvae are already developing in queen cells is to form a nucleus that includes a queen.

Ready an empty nucleus box and a queen or hatching cage (see pages 31 and 32). Find the queen, and lock her into the cage, which you attach to a brood comb with some wire or a rubber band. Hang the comb, along with the queen cage, into the nucleus box. Then take two or three brood combs from the colony that is in a swarming mood, break the queen cells out of them, and put them into the nucleus box. Shake the bees off two or three other brood combs into the nucleus box as well. Then release the queen from her cage.

If you have movable-frame hives, place a cover on the nucleus box. With a leaf hive, place the heating pad into the empty honey chamber of the new hive and block about three-fourths of the entrance by stuffing crumpled paper into it. Now take the nucleus to its new location. You must gradually add more empty combs to give the growing colony room to expand. If the colony is fed regularly (about a pint of sugar syrup daily, made up of equal parts sugar and water or 2 pounds of bee candy once a week), the nucleus will develop into a viable colony by fall.

You also have to remove the queen cells from all the brood combs in the original colony. To make sure you are not overlooking any, you must brush the bees off the comb into the hive body before you examine each comb.

After you break out the queen cells, the hive bees immediately start building new ones that must also be removed after nine days, leaving one or two. Be careful not to jolt the comb this time when you remove the queen cells because the future queen may fall off the royal jelly (see photo on page 38) and die. You should check after three weeks to see if there is a new queen in the colony and if she has started laying eggs.

If you find no sign of eggs or a queen, you have to test whether the colony is queenright. Hang a small piece of comb with eggs up to three days old (cut from the comb of another colony) or an entire comb with eggs and young larvae up to three days old into the hive. Mark the comb with a thumbtack.

Care and Management

If the colony is queenless, the bees will enlarge some of the cells into queen cells.

If that happens, place a small nucleus with a mated queen (see page 34) into the hive. (You should always have such a nucleus in reserve.) The comb with the eggs and the started queen cells must be removed first.

There are two more methods to prevent swarming: forming an artificial swarm and forming a brood nucleus. Since both methods require mated queens, however, I describe them in connection with rearing queens (see the next column) rather than here.

How to Deal with a Swarm

In spite of all the precautions you take, a colony will inevitably swarm now and then (see page 7). Once you have found the swarm—usually it has attached itself to the branch of a nearby tree—and want to determine which hive it has come from, you dust the cluster with some flour. Some of these "white" bees will fly back to their original hive, which you now move to another location.

Wet the swarm on all sides by spraying it with water from a fine nozzle. Be careful: If the swarm is too high to reach from the ground, make sure the ladder you use is on firm footing.

Now hold the swarm-catching box or basket (get the proper kind from a bee supply house)—if it is not raining even a sturdy cardboard box will do—and shake the branch from which the bees are hanging. If the branch is too big to shake, you can dislodge most of the cluster with a brush. Leave the box or basket with the bees in it on a stand or stepladder underneath the branch from which the cluster was hanging.

By evening all the bees will have moved into the catching container, and you will be able to transfer them into a new hive by giving the box or basket a good shake. With a movable-frame hive, you take out some of the combs, shake the bees in from the top (see page 22), and then replace the frames. With a leaf hive you work from behind. Attach the tray in back, and move the bees onto it by turning the catching box upside down and whacking it once or twice. The bees will immediately start crawling into the new hive. Then move the hive with the swarm to the spot where the old colony from which the swarm took off was located.

Rearing Queens

When you want to form an artificial swarm (see page 33) or a brood nucleus (see page 34), or if you want to requeen an old colony (see page 34), you need young queens. This is why you should rear some in June and July. You will need a box for an artificial swarm (a wooden box with a slot in the top

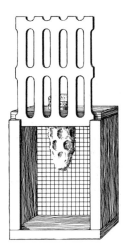

Hatching cage with a queen cell in it. One wall of the cage has a grate that can be pulled up. Nurse bees can pass through the slots to feed the hatched queen. The queen is too big, however, and cannot escape. The queen cage can also be used to store a queen temporarily (protective confinement).

into which a funnel is inserted), an empty frame modified with three slats running lengthwise along the center to create a long chamber, and one hatching cage (see drawing on page 31) per queen. You also need a "one-comb mating box,"—a small box made of Styrofoam or wood.

The sealed queen cells are placed in the hatching cages—one per cage—two to three days before the queens are due to emerge (the development period from egg to adult insect is 18 days). Dribble a small emergency ration of honey into the small hollow in the bottom of the cage that is designed for this purpose. Now place the hatching cages in a row in the long chamber of the modified empty frame and place the frame in the honey chamber.

Once the queens have hatched, sweep about as many young bees as will fit into a 1-pound honey jar from fully occupied combs (taken from one or more colonies) into the funnel of the box for the artificial swarm. You must do this slowly so that the older bees have a chance to fly off.

Then take a honey jar full of bees from the box for the artificial swarm and pour them into a mating box. Do this for as many boxes as you are going to use. Then close the lids and the entrances of the mating boxes. After about an hour you can let the queens enter through the entrance holes. Place the mating boxes into a cool, dark, but well-ventilated room (a cellar) for two days. Then, in the evening, move the mating boxes outdoors and open the entrances. Within the next two weeks the young queens will mate and prepare to start laying eggs. They are now ready for use.

If you have a Kirchhainer mating box you can use it over again after two or three days, placing new queen cells or virgin queens in it. This saves you and the bees time. The "one-comb boxes" can be used only once.

Marking the Queen

To make it easier to find a queen and to check her age, queens are marked with five different colors

Queen cage used for mailing and to introduce queen into nucleus (above). Before the queen is introduced into the hive or nucleus, the perforated section on the narrow side of the cage is broken out. The queen, along with a few bees from her colony, is placed in the larger compartment, and the smaller compartment is filled with bee candy. This way queens can be mailed in regular envelopes. The cages are thin enough to fit between the combs in the hive. A queen-catching glass (below). The bulging end of the glass tube is inverted over the queen on the comb. As soon as the queen has moved into the tube, close off the open end with a foam rubber plug. If the queen is to be isolated, rest the tube on the open queen cage, remove the foam plug, and blow the queen gently into the cage.

(one for each successive year) as soon as they have mated. You can buy marking sets including all the accessories (tiny, colored, plastic disks, also available numbered from 1 to 99, and glue) from bee supply firms.

As a new beekeeper you should employ a marking tube (available for about $3 or $4) to label your queen. Place the queen in this tube, and carefully push her with a movable plunger against the wide mesh at the end of the tube. Dab a tiny drop of glue onto her thorax through a hole in the mesh. Then pick up a colored plastic disk with the moistened end of a matchstick and lightly press it against the queen's thorax (see drawing on page 33).

Care and Management

If you practice marking drones, which do not sting and are somewhat larger than bees, you will soon get good enough at it to hold a queen between your fingers for the marking procedure. The colors of the disks conform to international norms and always follow the same order:

1986	1987	1988	1989	1990	1991 . . .
white	yellow	red	green	blue	white . . .

Clipping a Queen's Wings

As soon as the queens have mated, you should cut back one wing with sharp nail scissors to about half to a third of its original length. This is especially important if you cannot check your bees frequently. This way, if a colony swarms, the queen can fly only a few yards and will then drop to the ground, where a handful of bees will stay and protect her. The rest of the swarm returns home without the queen, and you will be able to find the queen with her attendants even days later. If she is marked, preferably with a numbered disk, you will know which colony she came from.

Introducing a Queen into an Artificial Swarm

Creating an artificial swarm is also a good method of preventing swarming when the woods are not producing honeydew (see page 9).

What you need for this is a box for an artificial swarm, that is, a box with a lid to which a hatching cage with a queen inside it is attached. Pour about 15,000 bees (3 pounds) from brood and honeycombs with plenty of workers on them—but no queen—into the funnel of the box. The bees will cluster inside the box.

Place the box into the cellar, and feed the bees. You can give them a pint of sugar syrup (mixing equal amounts of sugar and water, e.g., 1 quart of water to 2 pounds of sugar). Place the syrup in a glass jar, cover it with a piece of linen, and set it upside down on the bunghole of the box. The linen keeps the sugar solution from dripping into the box but allows the bees to suck it through the cloth.

Device for marking queens. Use the foam rubber plunger to push the queen carefully up to the grate of the device. Push her close enough that she can no longer move. Then dab a little glue on her thorax, and stick a disk with the year's color onto the glue.

After two days you transfer the artificial swarm into a new hive. Replace the plug of the hatching cage with one of bee candy. Use a piece of Apifonda about the size of a pigeon egg, or make your own bee candy by mixing one part honey with three parts powdered sugar. Then hang the queen cage between two combs. The bees will eat the candy, thus releasing the queen.

If there is no honey flow, the artificial swarm must be fed a pint of sugar syrup (composed as described above) every two or three days or 2 pounds of bee candy per week (see page 41).

33

Care and Management

Introducing a Queen into a Brood Nucleus

Introducing a queen into a brood nucleus is also a good way to forestall swarming. What you need for this are a queen in a hatching cage, an empty hive body (for movable-frame hives) or a nucleus box (for leaf hives), a food comb (that is, a comb that is largely filled with honey but has no brood) from another colony, an empty comb, and a frame with foundation.

Before noon on a good foraging day, remove two or three brood combs without the queen from a strong colony and combine these combs with the food comb, the frame with foundation, and the empty comb that you have sprayed with a little water. Place all these combs in the empty hive body or nucleus box. In the evening, hang the queen cage with the queen in it between two brood combs. Wait 24 hours, and then replace the plug of the queen cage with one of bee candy. The bees will eat the candy and thus release the queen. If you are working with a nucleus box, the nucleus must be moved to a hive after three or four weeks.

Replacing Queens in Old Colonies

If you want to replace the old queen in a colony, you must be certain that the bees are not in a swarming mood. A queen introduced at such a moment would instantly be killed by the bees. Reasons for replacing an old queen are:
• A queen should never be kept more than three years because a colony with an older queen is likely to lose strength. The time to replace an old queen is August or September.
• If the brood nest shows gaps or remains small, it is usually because the queen is missing a fore or hind leg and can no longer hold on properly to the edges of the cells when laying eggs. In this case, requeening is the only solution.

• If the bees sting more than usual even with proper handling, the genetic makeup of the queen is probably to blame. Here, too, requeening can help. There are several methods of replacing queens.

Requeening a Colony That is Left Queenless for Nine Days

Remove the old queen along with two or three brood combs from a hive to form a nucleus (see page 30). The queenless bees left in the hive will build queen cells, which you break out after nine days. The bees will get restless three or four hours later because in the course of the nine days all the cells were sealed and there is now no longer any possibility of rearing new queens. Place your new queen in the nucleus box after plugging the opening of her cage with bee candy (see left).

In the fall you can dispose of the old queen by squashing her against the frame with your thumb. The brood combs of the nucleus can be added to weak colonies.

When you requeen a colony that has been queenless for 9 days, the queen is usually accepted without problems, but there is a period of 10–12 days during which no new brood is produced.

Quick Requeening

The two methods described below can be used only before and after swarming season.

Lock the old queen in a queen cage, which you then hang between two brood combs. The next day you remove the old queen and substitute a new one but leave the cage in place. After another day you replace the plug of the queen cage with bee candy.

If you want to requeen in one day, you must follow another procedure for which you need a small wooden frame with plastic or wire screening (available from bee supply houses).

Remove the old queen from the colony. Brush the bees from a light-colored comb with hatching larvae, and set the new queen on it. Press the screen frame over the queen and into the wax deep enough to leave about ¼–⁵⁄₁₆ inches (6–8 mm) between the screen and the comb. In the piece of comb underneath the screen about two-thirds of the bees should have hatched but no new eggs should have been laid in the empty cells. Some cells must also be filled with honey. The bees that hatch from the remaining larvae will soon look after the new queen, which can then start laying eggs. The bees will chew a hole through the wax comb through which they and the queen can pass. Wait at least 10 days before you check to see if the bees have accepted the queen and if there are eggs and young brood. If there are no eggs or new brood, test to see if the queen is still present (see page 34). This method of requeening is not as reliable as requeening bees that have been left queenless for nine days.

Controlled Breeding and Artificial Insemination

Controlled breeding and artificial insemination are basically of interest only to apiarists who have years of experience and are working on a large scale, but I mention these procedures at least briefly because they are of crucial importance in keeping certain races and strains of bees purebred.

To achieve controlled breeding, bee breeders set up special breeding sites. In a wind-protected location, a clearing in the woods, for instance, a few colonies of drones are set up and fed. Within a radius of 4 miles or so (6–7 km) only bees of the same race are kept. Breeders bring their queens in mating boxes attended by some worker bees.

Artificial insemination is done under the microscope with an instrument that is especially designed for this purpose.

Harvesting Honey

Where the honey flow comes early, the beekeeper can expect to harvest the first honey in early June. In areas where the flow comes later, honey is ready for harvest two to four weeks later.

Removing the Honey

The best time to remove the honey from the hive is the late morning. Place next to the hive an empty hive body (for a movable-frame hive) or (for a leaf hive) a transport box that can be closed and some cloths or boards for covering exposed honeycombs. Then remove from the hive the combs that are completely or partially capped. Sweep the bees that are on the combs into the open hive or, in a leaf hive, onto the tray in back so that they can return immediately to their colony.

The job is easier if you can get the bees out of the honey chamber through a bee escape (an opening through which bees can move in only one direction). Close off the honey chamber from the brood chamber with a separator board. When the bees find themselves queenless, they seek a way to return to their queen. A bee escape in the separator board allows them to rejoin her but prevents them from getting back into the honey chamber. In two or three hours all the bees will have vacated the honey chamber. Of course, all the brood that was in the combs when you moved them into the honey chamber (see page 26) must have hatched by the time you want to remove the honey or the scheme will not work. This method is not only less arduous for you than sweeping the bees off the combs, but it is also easier on the bees.

If two-thirds of a honeycomb is sealed, it can be placed directly into the transport box that you have made ready. If you leave honeycombs standing around uncovered, foraging bees of the area will be attracted. Particularly at a time without honey flow, bees from other colonies—having learned of this free food source by their scouts—can quickly appear and cause fights around the honeycombs. This not only interferes with your work and upsets the colonies, but it can also be a serious nuisance for nearby neighbors because the bees start looking for food at all the windows, both open and closed.

Care and Management

If the combs you take out of the honey chamber are only partially capped, you must test the consistency of the honey that is not yet sealed. Take a comb and either hold on to the sides of the frame with both hands, shaking it up and down vigorously, or hold the comb with one hand and knock against the frame with your other hand. If honey comes spurting out of the cells that are still unsealed, the comb must be returned to the honey chamber and you must wait a few days before you extract the honey.

Extracting the Honey

The centrifugal extraction of honey is done in a room that can be kept free of bees. In addition to the extractor you need an uncapping tray, an uncapping fork, a double honey strainer, and a honey bucket.

Wear a clean, preferably white coat and headgear when you extract honey, and don't smoke. Honey is a food of high quality. It should go without saying that no pets are permitted in the extracting room.

First you remove the wax caps of the honey cells over the uncapping tray with the aid of the uncapping fork (see photo on page 28). Once both sides of the comb are uncapped, you place the comb into the basket of the extractor. Check to make sure that the lower edge of the comb always points toward the center of the extractor.

A honeycomb that has sealed honey cells on both sides may contain as much as 4 or 5 pounds of honey and is quite heavy. To prevent the breaking of combs, you should start the extractor basket moving slowly. The extractor can be powered by hand or by electricity. When some of the honey has been extracted, turn the combs around and extract honey from the other side. Start slowly again, and increase the speed of rotation after a few minutes. Keep spinning the combs until no more honey flows from them, and then turn them around once more and spin the other side (the one you started with) empty. This time you can start spinning fast right away.

The honey is pulled out of the cells by centrifu-

gal force and spun against the walls of the extractor. It runs down the walls and collects on the conical bottom of the extractor and then flows through a cock into a double strainer. This strainer consists of two steel sieves, one coarse and the other fine. Wax particles and foreign objects are blocked, and the pure honey collects in the honey bucket.

To get rid of the last bits of wax and other small foreign items, the honey should be filtered through a cloth filter (fine cheesecloth, available from bee supply firms) while still liquid, that is, right after having been extracted.

Then let the honey settle for a day or two at room temperature. Tiny air bubbles gradually rise to the surface, where they, along with some remaining wax particles that were not filtered out, form a layer of foam that should be skimmed off with a spoon or, even better, a spatula.

Depending on its composition and the plants from which the nectar was collected, honey crystallizes slowly or more quickly. For the crystallization to be uniform, the honey should be stirred but without mixing air into it. If the honey is not stirred, the crystals that form are uneven in size. This does not affect the quality of the honey in any way, but it changes its appearance and also can cause it to become rock hard. Honey generally crystallizes from the bottom up and from the walls toward the center.

As soon as the honey starts to look opaque—because millions of tiny crystals are forming—you should stir it carefully for about five minutes once a day for several days. Use a three-sided stirrer made of beech or oak wood (about 2 inches in

Above: Passing on food. The scent and the taste of the food source are absorbed by the receiving bee, and the round or wag-tail dance provides further information concerning the location of the food source.
Below, left: Field bee with pollen pellets in the baskets of her hind legs. Right: Fanning bee. The fanning regulates the temperature inside the hive and also spreads the colony's characteristic scent to all the inmates.

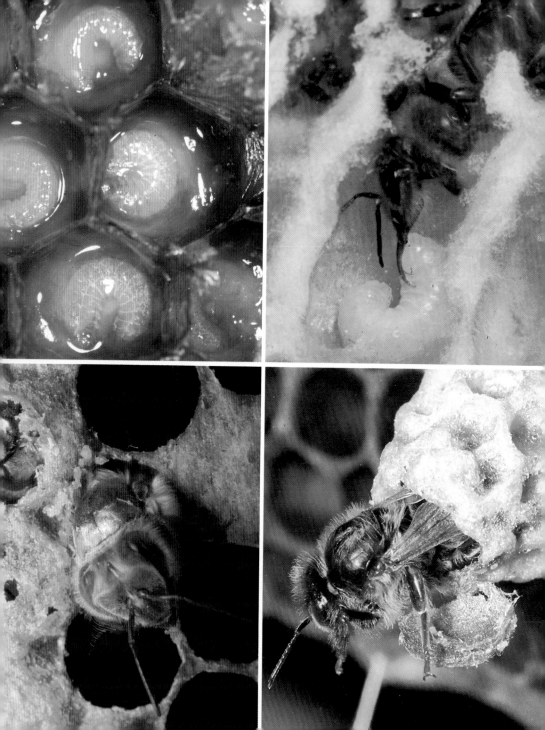

diameter and 3 feet long; see drawing on page 21). To provide a good grip, the upper third of the stirrer should be rounded.

If you have several buckets of honey to stir, you can use an electric drill equipped with an adapter (available from bee supply firms) and a honey stirrer made of metal. The adapter allows you to gear down the drill's speed to the much slower speed required for stirring honey.

Forest honey and honey from evergreen trees don't start crystallizing until much later, often not for months or even years after harvest. These kinds of honey therefore don't need to be stirred.

Packaging and Storing Honey

You can package honey for sale in large buckets or assorted retail-sized glass, tin, or plastic jars. For consumer-size packages (under 4 pounds or 1 gallon), the label should include the beekeeper's name, the declaration of net quantity of contents in ounces (with identification of weight of fluid measure), followed by the weight in pounds if the contents exceed 1 pound or 1 pint, and the beekeeper's control number.

If the honey has crystallized during storage, it must be liquefied before packaging. Heat the honey, but not above 104°F(40°C) because the quality of the honey suffers if it is overheated. You can melt the honey either in a thermostat-controlled heating cabinet (homemade or available for about $200 to $300 from beekeepers' supply firms) or with an electric immersion heater, also equipped

with a thermostat (cost about $300). The immersion heater can be placed directly on the solidified honey. Since jars and buckets are usually of uniform weight, you need to weigh only one jar and enter the tare in the scale before you fill and weigh all the jars of that size.

The packaged honey should be stored in a cool, dry room at about 60°F(15°C) until it is sold (see Different Kinds of Honey, page 52).

Honey for the Bees' Use and Interim Feeding

July is often a hard month for bees. In areas with early honey flow the food sources tend to become sparser at this time, and in areas with late honey flow the honeydew (see page 9) from fir and spruce doesn't start flowing until mid-July at the earliest.

If the bees cannot find more food than they need for their immediate use, no honey is stored in the honeycombs, but the queen keeps laying and the colony stays healthy. When you weigh your hives, check to see if there is sufficient food. The hives will show neither a gain nor a loss of weight if the bees gather just what they need to survive.

If there is no natural food supply (loss of weight!), you must start interim feeding. Before you do, however, you must remove or close off the supers or honey chambers because:

• Supers or honey chambers are not needed since nature is no longer supplying food.

• Some of the substitute food you offer may be stored in the honey chambers and adulterate the honey that may yet be produced.

• If the hoped-for late honey flow fails to materialize—because of inclement weather—the fall brood nest can be started right now.

Until the honey starts flowing again, give each colony half a pint of sugar water (one part sugar to one part water) every other day or 2–4 pounds of bee candy every two weeks.

Above, left: Bee larvae, about four days old, surrounded by fluid food. Right: A nine-day-old, fully developed larva being fed by a nurse bee.
Below, left: A fully developed worker bee is hatching after 21 days. She is chewing through the cell cap and crawling out of her cell. Right: A queen hatching. On her left front leg one can clearly see the hooks that she will later use to hang onto the cell edges when she lowers her abdomen into the cells to lay eggs.

Care and Management

You can also feed diluted honey (half a pint every other day, honey and water mixed in equal parts), but use only honey from your own bees. If you use honey from other sources, the danger of introducing disease (foulbrood) is too great. You must also supply a pollen substitute (brewer's yeast or soy flour). This is particularly important for bees foraging in forests, where enough summer and fall blossoms are often not available for the bees (2 pounds of pollen substitute lasts for three to four weeks).

Since the limited availability of food offered by the beekeeper resembles conditions when the honey flow is too sparse to permit storing honey for future use, the bees tend to respond by raising new brood. Interim feeding can thus be regarded as a stimulus to increase population. If the natural food sources start flowing again, supers or honey chambers must be reopened (see page 26).

At times when natural food sources dry up, there is danger of robbing. Bees from other colonies or from neighboring apiaries may clean out all the honey from your hives. This is why you should take the following precautions:

- Don't leave honey or food combs exposed.
- Don't take too much time checking the colonies, and don't leave the hives open long.
- Don't spill any syrup; if some does spill, wipe it up thoroughly, down to the last tiny drop.
- Reduce the hive entrance by two-thirds; in nucleus boxes leave open only a small slit (⅜ × ¾ inch, 1 × 2 cm). The guard bees must be able to defend the entire entrance.
- Don't feed liquid food until the evening when the bees have stopped flying.

Management of Weak Colonies

Don't try to winter over a weak colony; it is bound to die before spring. If you have two weak colonies, one with a good and one with a poor queen

(too old or damaged, or that is likely to produce bees that sting, see page 34), combine the two colonies in August. Find the undesirable queen and dispose of her (see page 34). In a movable-frame hive, place the hive body with the queenless bees either on top or underneath the colony with a queen. In a leaf frame, hang the combs with the queenless bees next to the bees with a queen.

If you have two weak colonies with poor queens, kill both the queens (see page 34) and add the brood combs to a mediocre colony that has a good queen.

Rearranging the Combs

In the fall the bees occupy only those combs on which several broods have been reared. This is why you must rearrange the combs in July or August. Remove all the light-colored combs that don't have brood in them as well as any foundations without drawn combs.

Hold old combs that have had brood in them several times against the sun or a bright light and see if any light shows through. Each emerging bee leaves a thin film of cocoon behind in the cell, and if there are enough of these cocoon layers that the light is no longer visible, the cells are too small for new brood. Cut dark combs (combs that block the light) out of the frames and melt them in a solar wax melter or exchange them for foundation. Light combs that are still diaphanous should be stored together with foundations until spring in hive boxes or a special comb-storage cabinet.

If any drone combs are present (combs made up entirely of drone cells, see page 6), these too should be removed.

Feeding to Stimulate Brood Production and Fall Feeding

For beekeepers in areas with early honey flow it is especially important to start the winter with

40

Care and Management

A solar wax melter that uses solar energy to melt old combs. The sun's rays, which hit the sloping glass top, heat the inside of the box to as much as 180°F (80°C), and a slate bottom stores the heat. Beeswax, which melts at about 150°F (65°C), drips into a receiving pan and hardens overnight.

strong colonies. Only strong colonies can take full advantage of the spring honey flow and collect an optimum amount of honey. In areas where the honey flow comes early one cannot count on harvesting honey after the end of July. To encourage the bees to keep rearing brood, you should start feeding them after removing the supers (see page 40). There are three possible methods: you can give them half a pint of sugar water (one part sugar to one part water) every other day, you can feed them bee candy (2 pounds every two weeks), or you can give them half a pint of diluted honey (half honey and half water) every other day. (Make sure you use honey only from your own bees!) Continue the feeding until the end of August. If there are no natural pollen sources, you must also make ready some pollen substitute (see page 25).

In areas with late honey flow, feeding to stimu-

late brood production is usually not necessary because the woods normally provide food until August. (If there is no honeydew, you should of course start feeding to stimulate brood production.)

The nectar, honeydew, and pollen that the bees collect and store from August on (from natural food sources or food provided by the beekeeper) are not enough to carry them through the winter and into the spring, and you must help them with additional feeding.

You should start the fall feeding in early September (two weeks earlier at altitudes above 1500 feet, 500 m), whether the honey flow is late or early. Note: Forest honey must be extracted before it is given to the bees.

You must assess how much food the bees will need. A common estimate of the food needs of a colony wintering over in one hive box is 17–22 pounds (8–10 kg); bees wintering over in two hive boxes need about 33 pounds (15 kg).

You can determine approximately how much the bees have already stored for the winter by using the following information:

• A piece of comb measuring 4×4 inches (10×10 cm) contains about 12 ounces of food or honey.
• A comb in a Hoffman frame (usually $4\frac{1}{2} \times 16\frac{3}{4}$ inches, 11×42.5 cm) and with sealed cells on both sides holds about 4 pounds of food or honey.

Figure out how much food the bees are short by subtracting your estimate of how much the bees have already stored from the amount needed for survival (see above). If you use bee candy, however, you must give the bees about 10% more than the amount you calculated. The candy must be processed by the bees before it is ready for storage, an activity that requires energy, which has to be provided in the form of food.

If you have movable-frame hives, remove the cover and the plastic sheet and place an insulating cover of appropriate size and with a hole in it on top of the combs. This "bunghole" should be $3\frac{1}{4}$ inches (80 mm) in diameter. The bee candy is placed on

Care and Management

this hole, and an empty hive body placed over the cover with the candy. Or you can simply fold back a corner of the plastic and place the bee candy on the plastic, but this causes more loss of heat.

If you have a leaf hive, remove the combs in the honey chamber and the queen excluder. Place the cover with the bunghole directly on the combs of the brood chamber and the bee candy on the bunghole.

Or you can feed the bees a sugar solution made of three parts sugar to two parts water. The following table shows the proper mixing proportions in kilograms and liters:

Sugar (kg)	Water (liters)	Amount Produced (kg)
1	0.7	1.2
2	1.3	2.4
3	2.0	3.6
4	2.7	4.8
5	3.3	6.0

The sugar and water are mixed together, heated (but not boiled!), and stirred until the sugar is completely dissolved. Liquid food must be given to the bees in feed troughs or special feeders. The most common type of feeder for both movable-frame and leaf hives is a 5 liter jar with a cover made of a fine bronze mesh. The full jars are placed upside down on the bunghole above the brood combs. The force of the vacuum keeps the sugar water from pouring out but allows the bees to absorb it through the tiny spaces in the bronze mesh.

In addition to feeder jars there are also food troughs in drawers (holding between 5 and 6 liters) that fit exactly into the hive body on top of the brood chamber.

Leaf hives are available, with a feeding trough holding 1 liter built into the side wall.

The bees should be fed 1 liter of sugar water a day. The feeder must·be washed with clean, hot water after every feeding.

Here is an example of how the feeding works:

You estimate that a colony occupying two hive bodies has stored about 5 kg of food. Assuming that the bees need about 15 kg to make it through the winter, there is a shortage of 10 kg. By mixing 9 kg of sugar with 6 liters of water, you get 10.8 kg of winter food. If you feed liquid syrup, you can give each colony 1 liter a day or 5–6 liters per week.

Feeding the bees daily is more work than less frequent feeding, but the queen will lay more eggs. If you feed Candy for Bees, or Hard Candy for Winter (see page 00), start by putting half a 15 kg package on the bunghole. Depending on how much food you expect your bees to need, you can add more as needed later. Feeding bee candy always has the effect of stimulating brood production.

Regardless of your method of feeding and whether you rely on an early or late honey flow, the feeding should always be completed by mid-September. If you live at altitudes above 1500 feet (500m), the winter feeding should be completed by the first of September.

Important note: The last time you check your hives, you must ascertain if there is enough food to last the winter. All the combs occupied by bees should have at least two-thirds of the cells capped by the end of September or beginning of October; that is, they must be filled with food. If this is not the case, supply extra food in liquid form immediately.

Last Preparations for Winter

After you have removed and cleaned the feeders, you should collect all the record cards in October. On days when the weather is above freezing and when there is only minor flying activity, you can repaint outdoor hives with an odorless paint that is safe for bees (buy the paint from a supplier of beekeeper's equipment). Make sure the covers fit tightly, and if necessary, make a tighter seal by fitting a sheet of clear plastic or a cloth of natural fiber over the hive body. If you have a leaf hive, install the insulating lid and check to make sure that the window to the brood chamber closes tightly. Drafts are harmful to bees, and the flight entrance provides enough air exchange for the hive.

Hives that are left outdoors must be covered with roofing paper that is weighed down with laths and rocks. To keep out mice, you should plug the entrance with blocks that have ½ inch slits in them or with wire screening. Both are available from suppliers of beekeeping equipment.

In the fall and winter, birds often catch bees that venture outside the entrance. To prevent this you can put netting in front of the hives. I myself don't use netting because so far I have found no evidence of birds preying on my bees. Often only those bees that are weakened by cold and have trouble returning to the hive are picked off by the birds.

Chores for Winter

You should inspect your hives periodically during the winter. Never open up the hives. Just look to see if the roofing paper has been damaged by storms and if the mouse blocks are still in place. Any damage should be fixed. Proceed quietly, and don't make knocking noises. On these inspection tours you will see many old, dead bees. Remove them carefully, but don't disturb the colony. Place a few of the dead bees in a small box, and keep them in a cool place until you can have them checked for nosema and acarine disease (see page 53) at your state testing laboratory (ask your beekeepers' association for the address).

Winter is the best time to build new hives and frames (see page 24). You can also repair equipment that is not in use at this time of year.

This is also the time to assemble all the current year's records you have entered on cards for each hive and analyze the information. This allows you to compare the performance of the different colonies. Keeping accounts (of expenses as well as income) shows you whether you have made a profit and how much.

If you keep your bees in a bee house, throw some cloths and blankets over the hives in February. The bees begin to forage for nectar and pollen (willow blossoms) in February and start a brood nest. For them to be able to maintain a brood temperature of 95°F (35°C), they need this extra insulation. Don't remove the covers until you open up supers for honey storage.

Spring Chores

As soon as the weather is warm enough in March, it is time for the first look into the hives:

Check to see if a functioning queen is present. A colony without a queen hums restlessly; fecal droppings are near the hive entrance, and there is no sign of brood. If this is what you find, the only solution is to combine the bees with a "queenright" colony, a colony with a queen (see page 34).

If you have a weak colony with a cluster only about the size of a fist and the combs are stained with droppings, the bees must be gassed. The bees are too few in number and too sick to survive, and if they were added to a stronger colony, they would endanger those bees' health. Light a piece of sulfur (available from suppliers of beekeeping equipment), replace the hive lid, and plug the entrance. The sulfuric gases kill the sick bees very quickly.

Check to make sure that the bees have enough food close to the brood nest. Full combs should be moved over to replace the empty ones near the brood nest. Don't forget to replace the insulating lid after your examination of the hive.

The next management chores are spring feeding and various measures to prevent swarming (see page 26).

The Bee Year at a Glance

1 Check the hive. **2** Keep mice out **3** Collect dead bees. **4** Repair storm damage. **5** Watch hive entrance. **6** First look into the hive. **7** Combine weak colonies. **8** Supply necessary warmth. **9** Feed pollen substitute. **10** Most important examination of the colonies. **11** Look for queen. **12** Add honey chamber or supers. **13** Place bees in nonswarming mood. **14** Retrieve swarms. **15** Prevent swarming. **16** Weigh honeycombs. **17** Uncap combs.

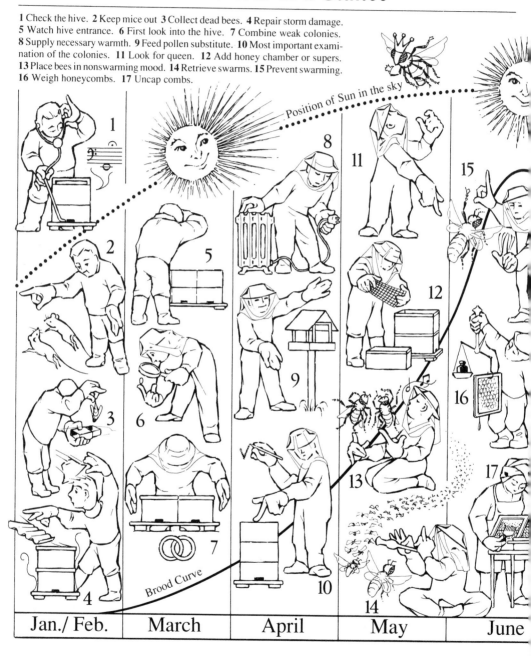

Position of Sun in the sky

Brood Curve

| Jan./ Feb. | March | April | May | June |

The Bee Year at a Glance

18 Raise new queens. **19** Prevent robbing. **20** Extract honey. **21** Supply plenty of pollen sources. **22** Start of new bee year. **23** and **24** Exchange queens. **25** check combs. **26** Supply winter food. **27** Last examination of the hive. **28** Cover hive. **29** Clean feeders. **30** Take precautions against mice and **31** birds. **32** Batten down winter roofing. **33** Last check. **34** Read bee literature. **35** Find buyers for your honey. **36** Make candles.

The Beekeeper's Yearly Work Cycle

In this chapter all the beekeeping chores are organized by the month in which they must be done. This work plan will guide you safely through the yearly work cycle (see also the drawing on pages 44 and 45).

What Needs to Be Done in January

The colony that is wintering over (there may be 10,000–20,000 bees) has contracted into a tight cluster that is distributed over four to eight combs. This cluster moves very slowly along the combs, usually in the direction away from the hive entrance. The bees are using up the winter food stored in the combs to be able to generate the necessary heat, that is, 68° to 77°F (20°–25°C) in the center of the cluster and 46°–50°F (80°–10°C) on the outer edges. A colony uses up about 20 to 25 ounces (600–700 g) of food per day in January.

By holding one end of a thin plastic or rubber tube against the hive entrance and the other against your ear you can hear the soft humming of the bees. Even a slight disturbance, such as a knock against the hive, will cause the sound to change, but the monotonous humming resumes when the knocking stops. When outside temperatures rise to between 50° and 54°F (10°–12°C), the bees take cleansing flights (see page 8).

• Look over your hives periodically, but only from the outside, to see if there is any storm damage.
• Check to make sure the mouse blocks are still securely in place in front of the hive entrance; a mouse invasion can be fatal for a colony wintering over.
• This is the time to repair hives and frames or build new ones.
• Analyze the entries on the record cards you have kept for the individual colonies (see page 43).
• This is also a good time to go to association meetings and workshops or lectures.
• During the winter months you have time to market your honey and find new clients or outlets.
• Note down on each colony's record card what you observe at the hive entrance. In January, for instance, you may find a number of dead old bees.
• If you have a scale hive, check its weight at the end of the month and compare the January weight with the December weight to see how much food was consumed. Make the appropriate entries on the record cards.

What Needs to Be Done in February

Although February counts among the winter months, some early spring flowers, such as snowdrops, may appear, and such shrubs as hazelnuts begin to produce the first pollen. The bees inside their hive also feel the life-giving warmth of the sun, and the queen begins to lay eggs. In the center of the cluster, a brood nest with eggs in the cells begins to form. It starts out about the size of the palm of your hand and gradually increases in size. As the bees eat more—in February they consume about 2 pounds (1000 g) of food a day—the temperature in the cluster rises from about 77°F (25°C) to 95°F (35°C).

Outdoor temperatures must rise to only 46°–50°F (8–10°C) for the first bees to venture out of the hive to gather water, which they need to tend to the brood. On some days it will also become warm enough for preliminary cleansing flights. If warm winds bring unseasonably high temperatures (57°F, 14°C and above), the hive's main cleansing flight can occur toward the end of February.

• Any neighbors living close to your hives should be informed in good time of the phenomenon of the bees' cleansing flights. Explain before the first warm days arrive that you cannot close off the hive entrance, because if you did, the bees would defecate inside the hive and the entire colony would die. Ask your neighbors not to hang out their wash on the first warm day but to dry it indoors. If the wash is hung outside it may well be spattered with little yellow dots. Bee spatters on a car can simply be washed off. If you explain politely just how important bees are for the pollination of plants, your neighbors will surely respond sympathetically.

• Check to make sure that the hives are tight (see page 25).
• Cover hives that don't have enough insulation (as in a bee house) with cloths.
• Check the hive's weight at the end of the month.
• Make the appropriate entries in the record cards.

What Needs to Be Done in March

In March the first catkins appear. These yellowish male flowers bear pollen that the bees carry to the greenish female flowers, pollinating them in the process. In warm weather, the female flowers are a good source of nectar. As larger amounts of pollen and nectar become available from willows, dogwoods, and other early-blooming plants, the hive becomes more and more alive. The bees need 3–4 pounds (1500–2000 g) of food a day during this month. The brood nest will by this time have spread out over three or four combs, and the population of the colony has started on its upward curve (see drawing on page 44).

As soon as the weather permits, it is time for the first examination of the colony:

• Check to see if the colony has a functioning queen (see page 30). If it does not, you must combine colonies (see page 30).
• A weak or sick colony must be gassed at this time (see page 58).
• Make sure there is enough food available close to the brood nest (see page 33).
• Check the hive's weight weekly now. Do it in the evening, after the bees have stopped flying.
• Make appropriate entries in the record cards.

What Needs to Be Done in April

By this time all kinds of willows are in bloom and, depending on the climate, poplars with red pollen, maples, beeches, oaks, sloe plum, currants, gooseberries, various kinds of cherry trees, and apple and pear trees. The variety of natural food sources and the fact that more and more pollen (protein) and nectar are needed for rearing brood motivate the bees to keep leaving the hive to forage for more food.

Within the hive a changeover of population is taking place. The old bees that wintered over are dying off, and young bees take their place. The brood nest has swelled to six or eight combs, and maintaining the brood temperature of 95° F (35° C) requires a great physical effort on the part of the house bees. In addition, major fluctuations in temperature pose a threat to the colony in April (see page 25).

• Attach the ramps below the entrances of the hives (see page 25).
• Keep insulating the hives if this is necessary (see page 25).
• If necessary, supply bee candy or sugar syrup (see page 25).
• If there is a long cold or rainy spell during which the bees cannot fly, you must give them pollen substitute (see page 25).
• If the bees occupy all the combs or are building combs in the building frame (in a leaf hive), it is time to expand their space (see page 26).
• Keep cutting out the comb in the building frame (see page 25).
• Check the hive's weight weekly.
• Make appropriate entries in the record cards.

What Needs to Be Done in May

By early May the colony has reached its full strength; 80% of the combs in the brood nest are filled with brood. The bees are at the height of their activity, and they are likely to want to swarm. It's your job to try to prevent the swarming impulse from arising or, if it does arise, to keep the bees from acting on it.

• Open up the honey chamber (see page 26).
• If the building frame in a leaf hive shows no sign yet of queen cells being constructed or queens being reared, you can shrink the colony (see page 29).

• As soon as workers start building queen cells, you must try to prevent swarming either by relocating the colony (see page 30) or by creating a nucleus with a queen (see page 30).

• If the bees swarm in spite of all your efforts, you must try to catch the swarm as quickly as possible (see page 31).

• If the bees have stored a lot of pollen, you may be able to remove a few combs filled with pollen and store them until fall, when they can be given back to the bees to build up their condition for winter.

• Check the hive's weight every week.

• Make appropriate entries on the record cards.

What Needs to Be Done in June

June brings the summer solstice, and the strength of the colony peaks during this month. The brood nest starts to get smaller because the queen is laying fewer eggs. There is still a danger of swarming, however.

The forests—both evergreens and deciduous trees—begin to produce honeydew from early to mid-June. The honeydew flow comes primarily from firs and spruces, but often other trees, such as oaks, maples, and pines, also produce honeydew (see page 9).

You can tell that the honeydew has started flowing when you see small, shiny droplets on the leaves of the underbrush. While the honeydew lasts, colonies can gain as much as 4 or 5 pounds (2 kg) per day (measured in a scale colony).

• In areas with early honey flow you may be able to harvest your first honey in early June (see page 35). If the flow continues to be strong, you may be able to extract honey again two or three weeks later. Where the honey flow is late, the first harvest can be expected at the end of June.

• June is the best month for rearing new queens (see page 31). As soon as the queens have mated, they should be marked (see page 32) and their wings clipped (see page 33).

• Continue to take measures to prevent swarming (see page 26). If you are rearing queens, creating an artificial swarm or making a brood nucleus are good ways to forestall swarming.

• Check the colony's weight daily.

• Make appropriate entries in the record cards.

What Needs to Be Done in July

After the summer solstice the bees enter their declining phase (see drawing on page 45). By the middle of July the danger of swarming is past. Colonies that have a young, healthy queen drive away the drones (see page 7). From mid-July on you can expect firs *(Abies alba)* to start producing honeydew.

• Continue measures to prevent swarming until the middle of July (see page 26).

• Rear a late crop of queens.

• If necessary, get ready to requeen colonies during the second half of July (see page 34).

• Where the honey flow is late, you may be able to take a second honey harvest in mid to late July.

• If nature doesn't offer enough food, you may have to resort to interim feeding (see page 39).

• Make sure the bees get enough pollen (see page 40), especially if they forage in the forest; put back the combs full of pollen that you removed in the spring.

• Take precautions against robbing (see page 40).

• Check over the combs; rearrange the brood nest and remove unneeded combs (see page 40); store light colored combs in your comb storage cabinet.

• Cut out dark combs and combs with drone cells; melt them down, or exchange them for comb foundation (see page 41).

• Check the weight of the scale colony daily.

• Enter appropriate data on record cards.

What Needs to Be Done in August

August is the beginning of the bees' new year. During this month the next winter's bees hatch (see page 7). The more bees there are to winter over, the

August

better the chance that the colony will be able to maintain the necessary temperature inside the hive. The warmer the bees keep, the stronger the colony will be in the spring and the more bees will be able to collect nectar and honeydew to turn into honey.

- Last harvest of honey in areas with late flow.
- If you haven't done so yet, requeen old colonies (see page 34).
- If you haven't yet checked and reorganized the brood nest (see page 43), do so now.

Important Food Plants for Bees

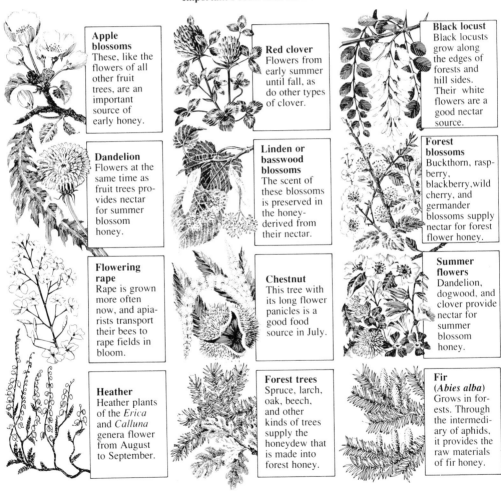

Apple blossoms
These, like the flowers of all other fruit trees, are an important source of early honey.

Dandelion
Flowers at the same time as fruit trees provides nectar for summer blossom honey.

Flowering rape
Rape is grown more often now, and apiarists transport their bees to rape fields in bloom.

Heather
Heather plants of the *Erica* and *Calluna* genera flower from August to September.

Red clover
Flowers from early summer until fall, as do other types of clover.

Linden or basswood blossoms
The scent of these blossoms is preserved in the honey-derived from their nectar.

Chestnut
This tree with its long flower panicles is a good food source in July.

Forest trees
Spruce, larch, oak, beech, and other kinds of trees supply the honeydew that is made into forest honey.

Black locust
Black locusts grow along the edges of forests and hill sides. Their white flowers are a good nectar source.

Forest blossoms
Buckthorn, raspberry, blackberry, wild cherry, and germander blossoms supply nectar for forest flower honey.

Summer flowers
Dandelion, dogwood, and clover provide nectar for summer blossom honey.

Fir
(*Abies alba*)
Grows in forests. Through the intermediary of aphids, it provides the raw materials of fir honey.

September–December

• Combine weak colonies (see page 34).
• At elevations above 1500 feet (500 m), feeding should start now, whether the honey flow is early or late. At lower elevations wait until early September (see page 36).
• As long as the bees collect nectar, weigh the scale hive daily; after the last honey harvest, weekly.
• Make appropriate entries in the record cards.

What Needs to Be Done in September

The colony will have gotten smaller because the old bees that die are no longer all replaced by young ones. As soon as the nights become cool, the bees in the hive contract into a cluster.

• By mid-September you should have finished feeding the bees, whether the honey flow is early or late in your area. At elevations above 1500 feet (500 m), the colonies should be all set for winter by early September.
•Take the empty combs on the sides of the brood nest out of the hive, and store them for winter.
• Examine the colonies for the last time before winter (see page 42).
• Wintering over two colonies, one on top of the other, is advantageous.
• Keep reading the scale weekly during the feeding period; afterward only monthly.
• Make appropriate entries in the record cards.

What Needs to Be Done in October

Late-blooming plants in gardens (asters) and in fields (field mustard) offer the bees some pollen to help cover the need for protein during winter.

• Remove and clean the feeders.
• On frost–free days and when few of the bees are out flying, hives set up outside can be given a new coat of paint (see page 42).
• Check to make sure the hives are tight, and seal cracks if necessary (see page 42). Supply insulation, and cover the hives with roofing (see page 43).
• Take precautions against mouse invasions: Reduce the size of the entrance, or attach mouse screens (see page 43).
• Put up bird nets if you wish (see page 43).
• Weigh the hive at the end of the month.
• Make entries in the record cards, and collect the cards of all the colonies.

What Needs to Be Done in November and December

The bees have by now contracted into a tight cluster. In order not to starve or freeze to death they must keep eating the sugar syrup they have stored in the combs in the fall. The carbohydrates contained in the sugar are converted to heat.

• Check the hives once or twice a month, but be sure not to open them up (see page 43).
• Build new hives and other equipment; do whatever repair work is necessary.
• Combine and analyze the data on the record cards (see page 43).
• Expand your theoretical knowledge about bees and beekeeping. (See the list of useful books and other publications on page 65).
• Work on marketing your honey.
• Make use of the beeswax (for candles).

Products of Beekeeping

Honey

Honey is an easily digestible food that contains many substances (vitamins and trace elements) that are valuable for the human organism. The Sumerians, Babylonians, and Egyptians knew that honey can act as a disinfectant and counteracts inflammation, and they made salves of it for the treatment of wounds and diseases of the eyes and the skin. Even today honey is still recommended as preventive medicine against infectious diseases and as an agent to speed the healing process. Chewing on honey and beeswax (comb honey, see below), for instance, helps relieve hay fever and chronic inflammations in the oral cavity.

Depending on the kind of nectar or honeydew the bees collect, different kinds of honey are produced that vary considerably from each other in color and taste. Some honeys consist primarily of nectar from one kind of plant, whereas mixed honey comes from a number of different plant sources (summer flowers, forest flowers, and forest trees). By analyzing the pollen present in the honey, it is possible to reconstruct which plants supplied the nectar. Many mixed honeys contain as many as 50 different kinds of pollen.

Comb honey is ripe honey stored by the bees in combs they have built but never used for brood rearing. The individual cells are capped with wax by the bees. The nectar for comb honey can come from any plant source.

The table on page 52 gives an overview of the different kinds of honey and what they look and taste like.

Wax

A colony that develops normally draws combs on 8–12 foundations during the time the nectar flows in one year. In the winter no wax is produced. At times when the colony is not functioning smoothly, as when the queen is old or sick or if no queen is present at all, less wax is produced. In the fall, when the beekeeper has rearranged the combs (see page 50), the wax—from four or five combs per colony—can be sold.

Pollen, Royal Jelly, and Propolis

Pollen is a highly nutritious food used in various diets. The pollen is collected with the aid of a pollen trap. (Beekeepers' suppliers sell pollen traps as well as the necessary materials and instructions for building them yourself.) The device works as follows: The bees are forced to pass through a small opening at the entrance. The opening is just large enough to let the bees through but strips off the pellets of pollen on the bees' legs. The pollen drops through a wire grate into a receptacle below, which must be emptied every day. The pollen should be dried as quickly as possible.

Some authorities recommend that people should eat 1–2 teaspoons of pollen a day for two to three months every year.

Royal Jelly is the food that nurse bees secrete for feeding queen larvae (see page 6). The usefulness of this substance for human consumption is debated, and therefore there is little market for it.

Propolis is plant resin that the bees collect from plant buds and mix with enzymes (produced by the bees) and with wax and pollen. It is used in the preparation of medicines because of its antibacterial effect. Bees cover all parts of the hive with a thin layer of propolis for disinfecting purposes, sealing any cracks and holes, and they also use it to reduce the size of the entrance for winter. You can scrape off the propolis on the inside walls of the hive and on the frames and sell it.

Products of Beekeeping

Different Kinds of Honey

Kind of honey	Origin	Taste	Color when freshly extracted	Color when crystallized
Dandelion honey	Dandelion	Strong and aromatic	Yellow	Bright yellow
Rape honey	Rape	Mild characteristic flavor	Light yellow	Whitish
Clover honey	Red, white, sweet yellow, vetches	Mild	Yellow to brandy colored	Whitish yellow to gray
Basswood honey	Basswood trees (nectar and honeydew)	Very aromatic, characteristic flavor	Greenish to yellow	Greenish gray
Chestnut honey	Chestnut trees	Distinct, somewhat tangy flavor	Amber	Golden to gray
Black locust honey	Black locust	Mild	Translucent	Whitish to greenish gray
Fruit blossom honey	Fruit trees and berry bushes	Mild	Light to golden yellow	Light to golden yellow
Summer blossom honey	All nectar-bearing flowers of summer	Aromatic	Golden yellow to brandy colored	Whitish to golden yellow, slightly grayish
Forest blossom honey	Willow, raspberry, blackberry, germander, buckthorn, horse chestnut (honeydew)	Mildy spicy	Golden yellow to amber	Yellowish gray
Forest honey	Spruce, oak, maple (honeydew)	Mildy spicy	Amber to reddish brown	Golden to amber
Heath honey	Heath plants	Very aromatic characteristic flavor	Reddish yellow to amber	Retains jellylike consistency for a long time
Fir honey	European white fir (honeydew)	Mildy spicy	Greenish black	Grayish brown

Diseases, Pests, Dangers

If you let the bees draw new combs from foundations (see page 26) every year for the brood nest—or, better yet, for the entire brood chamber—pathogens will have very little chance to establish themselves in your hives. In spite of this precaution and in spite of conscientious care, however, diseases may invade your colonies. To learn how to recognize and counteract diseases in the hives and to get some practical experience in dealing with them, you should take some courses on this topic. Beekeepers' associations and extension agents (see page 67) will be able to inform you about when and where courses on bee and brood diseases are offered.

As soon as you suspect disease in your hives, you must immediately notify the expert on bee diseases in your beekeeper's association. This person and, if necessary, the official state veterinarian, will diagnose the disease and tell you whether the disease must be reported and what treatment is recommended or mandated.

Diseases of Adult Bees

Acarine Disease:
This must be reported!

The mite *Acarapis woodi* penetrates into the tracheae of bees one to eight days old and bites through the tracheal walls to suck the bees' blood. In the process, blood enters the tracheae, where it coagulates and clogs the air passage. The bees cannot absorb enough air and, unable to fly, they merely hop in front of the hive.

Prevention: Keep your colonies strong and the population renewing itself rapidly.

Treatment: Should be treated by an official member of an apiculture research branch or of your local county agricultural extension service.

Varroatosis: This must be reported!

The mite *Varroa jakobsoni* was first found by Jacobson in Java in 1904 as a parasite on Indian bees. This mite lives on the surface of adult bees and on brood and feeds on their body fluids. A number of non-European bee races have existed with this ectoparasite for decades, without their health being significantly affected. For European bees, however, and that includes the carniolan bee, varroa mites represent a deadly danger. Colonies that are infested with this mite and are not treated die within four to five years.

The light brown mites are visible to the naked eye (females: oval, 1 mm long and 2 mm wide; male: roundish, with a diameter of approximately 0.8 mm). The varroa mite is often mistaken for the harmless bee louse *(Braula coeca)*. If you use a magnifying glass you can easily distinguish the two parasites: The mite has eight legs, the louse, only six (see drawing below).

Treatment: In the United States various chemicals for treating varroatosis are given (in controlled amounts) in the spring and fall: Phenothiazine, Napthalene, Varroazin, Tedion and Folbex. The expert on bee diseases for your beekeeper's association can also advise owners of bees on the choice and proper use of medications.

A biologic countermeasure you can take is to cut out and destroy the combs containing sealed drone brood. Varroa mites prefer drone cells for reproduction.

Nosema Disease

The single-celled parasite *Nosema apis* is always present in the alimentary tract of bees. If a

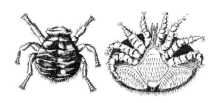

Bee louse (left) and varroa mite (right). It is easy to tell these two ectoparasites apart: The relatively harmless bee louse has only three pairs of legs, the dangerous varroa mite has four.

colony is weakened, individual bees are worn out from physical exertion, or if insufficient pollen (protein) is available, the parasites can multiply rapidly and destroy the cells of the bees' intestines. Infected colonies decline in the spring, the brood combs are no longer covered by bees, the temperature in the brood nest drops, and the larvae die. The sick bees are unable to fly; their abdomens are swollen, and they can be seen crawling around with trembling wings in front of the hive. You can tell if a bee died from nosema disease by pulling her intestines out of the abdomen and looking at them. In a healthy bee the intestines are reddish brown; in bees suffering from nosema disease, they are milky white.

Prevention: Take good care of your bees, and keep the colonies strong. Make sure, particularly in the fall, that the bees have enough pollen; if there is too little, supply pollen susbstitute (see page 25).

Treatment: You can treat nosema disease yourself. Fumidil B, an antibiotic drug made by Abbott Laboratories is mixed—following the instructions in the package exactly—into the sugar syrup or bee candy fed to the bees in the spring or late summer. This very effective drug is at the moment not available on the market because it is being tested once again. You can find out from your beekeeper's association when it will become available again.

A drug called Nosemac (made by Drageno Pharm and available from dealers in beekeepers' supplies) is also effective. This drug, too, is given in the spring or late summer in accordance with the directions that come with it. A normal package of 15 tablets is enough for five colonies.

Brood Diseases

You can spot brood diseases only if you know what *healthy brood* looks like:

Brood nest: Areas covered with brood should be interrupted by only very few unsealed brood cells.

Cells: The caps of the cells should be slightly convex and of a uniform light brown color.

Larvae: Plump, color of mother-of-pearl.

Odor: Odorless

European Foulbrood

Causative agent: The bacterium *Streptococcus pluton.*

Brood nest: Has gaps in the brood.

Cells: The cell caps are discolored, sunken, and punctured; inside the cells there are rubbery, brownish black, smooth scabs that the bees can easily remove during the early stages of the disease.

Larvae: Dark brown color, doughlike to sticky or slimy consistency. There are dead larvae in sealed as well as unsealed cells, usually lying in the lower part of the cell. If you do the match test,* no strings or filaments form.

Odor: Sour.

*Match test: Stick a match into a cell with a dead larva in it and pull it out again. Sacbrood and European foulbrood are often mistaken for American foulbrood. American foulbrood, which is far more damaging than the other brood diseases, is present only if the match pulls up stringy filaments from the dead larvae.

Treatment: The disease will subside on its own at the end of the brood season.

American Foulbrood: This must be reported!

Causative agent: The bacterium *Bacillus larvae* (spore bearing).

Above, left: A honeybee with pollen in her pollen baskets on a coltsfoot flower. Right: Bees on dwarf aster flowers (excellent source of pollen).
Below, left: A honeybee absorbing honeydew from spruce needles. Right: A carniolan bee (with gray bands on her abdomen) on a clover flower.

Brood nest: Gaps in the brood.
Cells: The cell caps are discolored, sunken, and punctured. In the bottom of the cells there are blackish brown scabs that resist removal by the bees.
Larvae: Light to dark brown and slimy. Dead larvae lie stretched out flat on the bottom of sealed and unsealed cells. If you do the match test, a stringy filament is pulled up by the match.
Odor: Glue-like.
Treatment: Treatment must follow guidelines issued by the state department of agriculture.

Chalkbrood

Causative agent: The fungus *Ascosphaere apis.*
Brood nest: Gaps in the brood.
Cells: Cell caps light or dark, some of them punctured.
Larvae: White, later grayish black, hard, and chalklike in consistency. Dead larvae in sealed cells. Odorless.
Treatment: The disease will subside on its own; cut out and burn infected combs.

Stonebrood

Causative agent: The fungus *Aspergillus flavus*
Brood nest: Has gaps in the brood.
Cells: Some caps are punctured; affected cells can look greenish and mildewy.
Larvae: Greenish yellow, hard, and shriveled; larvae cling to the cell edges; dead larvae in sealed and

unsealed cells.
Odor: Musty.
Treatment: The disease will subside on its own (bees chew off and dispose of the affected cells).

Sacbrood (rare)

Causative agent: A virus whose exact identity has not yet been established.
Brood nest: Gaps in the brood.
Cells: Cell caps are dark, sunken, and punctured; inside the cells there are yellowish brown or dark gray scabs that the bees can easily remove.
Larvae: Gray to black, watery and granular consistency; dead larvae in sealed and unsealed cells, usually with the head sticking straight up. No filament forms when you do the match test.
Odor: Sour.
Treatment: The disease subsides on its own.

Pests

Waxmoths lay their eggs on both combs in hives and on combs that have been removed for storage. The emerging larvae, which feed on wax, destroy the combs. A waxmoth infestation can easily be recognized by the fine gray webs with which the larvae have lined the paths they have eaten through the comb. In strong colonies, the bees keep the waxmoths under control by killing the emerging larvae and carrying them out of the hive.
Prevention: After removal from the hive of any combs you want to store in hive bodies or in a comb storing cabinet, you should fumigate them two or three times after removal from the hive at intervals of three to four weeks. (You can buy fumigants with directions on how to use them from suppliers of beekeeping equipment.) Store the combs at room temperature or, better, somewhat cooler.
Treatment: If you have a major waxmoth infestation, the nests must be burnt and the ruined combs with holes in them must be cut out and melted

Above: Movable-frame hives in a flowering rape field. Below, right: The honey chamber of an open movable-frame hive filled with white wax cells that are full of honey (containing a good 30–40 pounds (15–20 kg) of honey. This kind of harvest is proof that the beekeeper has treated the bees right. Right: The author is demonstrating how gentle his bees are. The larger cells house drone brood, the darker cells below, worker brood.

Diseases, Pests, Dangers

The bee louse (Braula coeca), an insect with six legs that is about 1–1.5 mm in diameter (see drawing on page 53), usually attaches itself to the thorax of a bee and takes food from its proboscis. On queen bees as many as 20 lice have been counted, although on worker bees they occur only singly. Bee lice don't do any direct harm, but they bother the bees. Queens infested with them slacken their egg laying.
Remedy: Slip a piece of paper with some naphthalene sprinkled on it into the hive underneath the combs in the evening. The naphthalene paralyzes the lice, and they drop down on the paper. The next morning remove the paper carefully. Promptly burn the paper with the lice on it.

Wasps usually pick off only sick bees or bees that are unable to fly off the landing board in front of the hive. In the fall, however, wasps also try to get at the honey inside the hive. The guard bees at the entrance can easily ward off individual wasps (see page 11), but when many wasps attack all at once, there is danger of robbing.
Remedy: Partially block off the entrances in the fall. In the spring you can place bulging bottles with narrow necks, filled up to a quarter with thin honey water or fruit juice, near the hives. The wasps are attracted by the sweet smell and drown in the liquid.

Hornets have become comparatively rare and therefore pose no threat to honeybees.

Burrowing wasps of the *Philanthus* genus also prey on bees near the hive entrance, but they don't pose a serious threat to the colonies.

Larder beetles (Dernoites ladarius) are sometimes found in neglected hives, usually in the debris (small wax particles from the caps that have been chewed off brood and honey cells) on the bottom board of the hive body. The larvae have tufts of long hair, and the blackish brown beetles have a gray cross stripe. The beetles bother the bees and disrupt the brood rearing.
Prevention: Keep the bottom board clean, and don't leave pieces of comb lying around.
Remedy: Collect all bits of wax, and melt them down. Clean out and burn any debris from the bottom of the hive body in the spring.

Ants can do quite a bit of damage by chewing through the hives and invading bee colonies.
Remedy: Put ant bait (available at drugstores or from suppliers of beekeeping equipment) in the hives (following the instructions of the product).

Mice tend to invade bee hives primarily in the fall and winter. A mouse nest in a hive is enough of a disruption for wintering bees that the colony usually perishes.
Prevention: Reduce the size of the entrances in the fall to a slot about ¼ inch (5 mm) wide, or install a mouse grate.

Birds don't do much harm because they usually eat only sick or dead bees. They can, however, be a serious nuisance in queen rearing if they catch young queens during their nuptial flight.
Remedy: Set up scare crows near the hives, or hang strips of aluminum foil on trees near the hives.

The Dangers of Pesticides and Herbicides

Pesticides represent a constant danger to honeybees. Bees that come in contact with a pesticide in the course of collecting nectar from plants die instantly or succumb on the flight back to the hive. If a forage crop has been treated with a pesticide, the colony becomes progressively weaker until the losses become too great for the colony to survive.

There are legal guidelines for the application of pesticides, specifying the degree of danger to honeybees. You can obtain this information from a number of sources, such as your beekeepers' association, the U.S. Department of Agriculture, and environmental protection agencies.

It should go without saying that you yourself should not use pesticides. Ask your neighbors and acquaintances to abstain from the use of pesticides, too.

Herbicides (chemicals used to control weeds) seldom kill honeybees directly but destroy many of the plants that are important food sources for honeybees. Help convince officials, as well as the public, that it is better not to destroy wild plants and "weeds" around the edges of fields, along road-sides, on the banks of rivers, and along the shores of lakes. If it is essential that these plants be removed, it can be done by mowing rather than by spraying.

If your colonies are suffering from poisoning through pesticides or herbicides, inform:
•the president of your beekeepers' association or his or her representative,
•the appropriate official of the state environmental protection agency,
•the person or company responsible for the damage, if known,
•the police in case of extensive damage.
Your beekeepers' association can supply you with information on how to get a sample to test the extent of poisoning. The association can also tell you how to prepare a report of the damage for your insurance company.

GLOSSARY

A Short Glossary of Beekeeping Terms

Afterswarm The portion of a colony that leaves the parent hive with one or more virgin queens.

Allergy Excessive physical sensitivity to bees and their venom; see page 13.

Apimondia International organization of beekeepers with offices in Bucharest and Rome.

Apis mellifera carnica Carniolan bees, a race that is especially gentle.

Antibiotics Substances that inhibit the growth of bacteria or kill them.

Bands, abdominal Dense bands of hair on the abdomen of bees. These bands are especially wide in carniolans, which is why these bees appear gray (see page 22).

Bee candy A mixture of powdered sugar and honey (proportions 3:1); also produced commercialy without honey, using an inverting enzyme as a softener (see page 41).

Bee candy plug The plug of the queen cage is replaced with a piece of bee candy about the size of a pigeon egg when the queen is introduced into a hive.

Bee escape A device that allows bees to pass through one way but not to return.
Beehive See *Hive*.

Bee house A protective structure for bee hives that is large enough for the beekeeper to enter and perform beekeeping chores inside it.

Bee language Gestures (dancing) through which information is communicated to members of the colony. This behavior was first discovered and described by Professor Karl Ritter von Frisch (1886–1982), who received the Nobel Prize for his pioneering research (see page 9).

Bee pasture Wild and cultivated plants, bushes, and trees that supply nectar, honeydew, or pollen.

Bee space A apace about $^3/_8$ inch (10 mm) wide through which bees can move freely. Bees tend to fill smaller spaces with propolis and build combs in larger ones.

Bee year Starts in August because bees hatched during this month are the ones that will rear the spring population.

Begging for entrance Bees not belonging to the colony trying to become accepted.

Bottom insert A piece of material, such as tar paper, that is slipped underneath the wintering colony and is removed in the spring with the debris that has collected on it.

Breeding stock Eggs or larvae form selected colonies used to breed queens with desirable traits.

Brood The offspring produced by the colony (eggs and larvae).

Brood nest All the combs of a colony with brood in them.

Builder bees Bees that sweat wax and build combs (see page 5).

Building cluster Young bees hanging on to each other in a cluster and producing wax from which they construct combs.

Building frame An empty frame, which the bees—depending on the colony's mood—fill with either worker or drone brood cells. If the bees start modifying regular cells into queen cells, this is a sign that the colony may be getting ready to swarm.

Carniolan See *Apis mellifera Carnica.*

Cellar detention Artificial swarms and mating boxes are kept in a cool room (approximately 60°F, 15°C) for two days to give the bees time to get used to the queen.

Cells Honeybees build wax combs made up of hexagonal cells for brood rearing and storage of honey and pollen.

Chitin The horny substance forming the exoskeleton of bees and other insects.

Cleansing flight Bees avoid defecating inside the hive. In the winter the waste collects in their intestines, and as soon as it is warm enough (50°–54°, 10°–12°C) the bees leave the hive to relieve themselves (See page 46).

Colonies, uniting Forming one strong colony out of two or more weak ones.

Colony, development of The brood-rearing phase starting after the winter rest and culminating around the summer solstice.

Colony, drone A colony of bees with an intentionally high proportion of drones.

Colony, queenless A colony without a queen.

Colony, queenright A bee colony that has a queen.

Colony, a shrinking Removing bees or brood combs from the hives to prevent swarming.

Combs Combs are made up of hexagonal cells (four per square centimeter) built at a slight upward angle.

Comb, age of If you hold a comb up against the sun or a bright lamp, some light should shine through. If it is completely opaque, the comb is too old and should be melted down.

Comb, egg A small piece of comb with eggs that is used for breeding purposes or to test for the presence of a queen (see page 30).

Comb, natural Combs built by bees without the aid of foundation (see *Foundation*).

Comb pliers Tool used with hives worked from the back (see drawing on page 21).

Comb, settling Sometimes a swarm of bees moves out of a hive to which it has been transferred because the bees don't feel at home there. A comb with brood in open cells, hung into the hive before the swarm is introduced, stimulates them to take care of the brood and helps the swarm settle down in the hive.

Combs, capping Bees seal cells that are filled with ripe honey with a thin wax cover to preserve the honey.

Combs, old Dark combs that have been used repeatedly for brood rearing. They should be cut out of the frame, melted down, and the wax exchanged for new foundation.

Combs, spacing of The space between combs is usually about $^3/_8$ inch (see *Bee space*).

Combs, trimming Cutting combs to fit into different frames.

Consolidation Removing combs not occupied by bees.

Crawling Bees that are unable to fly often crawl. Possible causes for crawling are acarine disease (see page 53), varroatosis (see 53), or poisoning. If crawling is observed repeatedly, have the hive inspected.

Debris Tiny bits of wax from the chewed-off caps of brood and honey cells that drop to the bottom of the hive.

Diseases, mandatory reporting of The presence of certain bee and brood diseases must be reported to state and/or federal government inspection offices (see page 65).

Drone Male of the bee.

Drone cell A brood cell that is larger (6.91 mm diameter) than the normal worker brood cells (5.37 mm) and in which the queen deposits drone eggs.

Drone congregating areas Geographically favorable spots that attract drones eager to mate with young queens.

Drone killing Expelling of drones in the late summer after the reproductive drive has passed and the drones are no longer of use to the colony.

Early flow area Area where the honey flow comes early, from March to about July.

Entrance An opening through which the bees can leave and enter the hive.

Equipment for harvesting honey See page 35.

Excluder grid A grate inserted between the brood chamber and the honey chamber with spaces wide enough (between ⅛ and ³⁄₁₆ of an inch, 4.3 mm) for the worker bees to pass through but not the larger queen.

Extracting room A work room that is bee proof.

Fanning Rapid beating of the wings near the entrance that causes air to move through the hive (ventilation).

Feeding, fall Replenishing the colony's food stores for the winter.

Feeding to stimulate brood rearing When there is no food from natural sources, the beekeeper must feed the bees so that they will carry on the brood business.

Flower fidelity Bees usually visit only one kind of flower on a foraging trip. This plays an important role in the preservation of the purity of species. Other insects move indiscriminately from flower to flower.

Field bee Bees are subject to a strict division of labor. During the first 12 days of life they work inside the hive; afterward they serve as field bees, collecting nectar, honeydew, and pollen (see pages 6 and 12).

Flight direction The direction in which the entrance points.

Flour test See page 31.

Forage bee See *Field bee.*

Foundation A thin sheet of beeswax with the honeycomb pattern for workers' brood cells embossed on it. The bees build or "draw" complete cells on both sides of the foundation.

Frame A wooden frame that holds comb foundation and is reinforced by wire (see *Foundation*).

Frame sizes The two frame sizes most commonly used in Germany are the German normal size, 37×22.3 cm, and the Zander size, 42×22 cm.

Frames, self-spacing These ensure that the frames hang or stand about ³⁄₈ inches (10 mm) apart (see *Bee space*).

Frame wire Wire used to reinforce frames to keep foundation from sagging.

Gassing Destroying a contaminated colony by burning sulfur.

Guard bees Worker bees that guard the hive entrance (see pages 7 and 11).

Hair Bees are covered almost completely with furlike hair. When they visit flowers, pollen sticks to the hair (see Feeding and Pollination, page 8).

Hive A wooden box in which bees live (see pages 16–20).

Hive bee Young worker bee up to 20 days old that works only in the hive (see pages 6 and 7). Also called house bee.

Hive body Part of a hive.

Hive, leaf A hive that is worked from behind. The frames rest vertically on a grate of metal bars, their ends toward the entrance. When one frame is removed, the others can be moved by flipping them like the pages of a book (see page 19).

Hive, movable-frame A hive composed of two or more stacked hive bodies (see page 16).

Hive scent All the worker bees of a colony produce a scent that is characteristic of their colony and is recognized by all the members (see *Smell, sense of*).

Hive tool A metal bar to loosen combs.

Honey See page 35.

Honey chamber A chamber, separated from the brood chamber by a queen excluder, with combs in which the bees store honey.

Honeydew A sweet liquid excreted by certain plant-feeding insects, such as plant lice (Aphididae), bark or scale insects (Coccidae), jumping plant lice (Psyllidae), and white flies (Aleyrodidae).

Honey, extracting See page 36.

Honey flow The period when the greatest amount of nectar is available within the bees' flight range.

Honey, kinds of See page 52.

Honey, leaf Honeydew from deciduous trees.

Honey, liquefying Gradual heating of crystallized honey up to 104°F (140°C).

Honey manipulation See page 35.

Honey stomach See page 8.

Humidity The relative air humidity inside a hive is about 60%. Higher humidity contributes to the spreading of disease and inhibits proper brood development; in the winter it can also cause mildew on the combs. To counteract rising humidity, consolidate the colony (see *Consolidation*).

Insemination, artificial Mechanical insemination with the sperm of selected drones. The queen is an-

esthetized with CO_2, and the procedure is performed under a microscope.

Interim feeding See page 39.

Lachnidae Family of aphids that feed on trees and produce honeydew.

Landing board A place where the bees can land in front of the entrance.

Larvae From the eggs the queen lays, larvae hatch that later pupate and eventually turn into adult insects (see page 6).

Late flow area Area where the honey flow comes late, usually from trees; generally from June to August.

Lecanidae Family of scale insects that produce honeydew.

Listening It is possible to hear the bees humming inside the hive in the winter (when the hive must not be opened) by taking a thin rubber tube and holding one end to the entrace and the other to your ear. The quality of the humming can give you important clues about the state of the colony.

Match test See page 54.

Mating The young queen takes several flights from the hive and copulates with five to eight drones, which die after the union. A queen stores between eight and ten million spermatozoa, enough to fertilize eggs for her entire lifetime.

Mating box Hive for a very small nucleus; point of departure for a young queen when she sets out on her nuptial flight.

Mating site A spot that is ideally situated for setting up mating boxes with selected drones for the purpose of planned breeding.

Medications See the chapter on diseases and their treatment, starting on page 53.

Microclimate Maintenance of temperature within the hive.

Mobbing A queen can be attacked by hostile bees that surround her in a tight mob. The queen is usually injured or killed.

Nectar A sweet liquid secreted by glands (nectaries) in the flowers of plants. The nectar is converted by the bees into honey.

Nucleus Part of an established colony separated from the main colony without the queen. As the word implies, a nucleus is the beginning of a new colony.

Nucleus box A small hive used for housing a small colony or nucleus.

Nuptial flight Mating flight.

Nurse bee Young hive bee (see pages 6 and 12) whose task it is to feed the larvae.

Orientation flights Short flights taken by workers that are about to start working as field bees to become familiar with the surroundings of the hive. Also called play flights.

Ovaries Only the queen has fully developed ovaries; worker bees have only rudimentary ovaries.

Oxygen, lack of If bees are transported in hives, a shortage of oxygen may arise and cause the death of the entire colony.

Pheromone See *Queen substance*.

Pollen analysis Examination of the various kinds of pollen contained in honey to determine the source of the honey.

Pollen substitute A food, such as soy flour, brewer's yeast, or fat-free milk powder, given to bees when their stores of pollen are low.

Pollen trap A grate through which the bees must crawl that removes the pollen pellets from their legs as they enter the hive.

Propolis See page 51.

Queen See page 5. The queen determines the activities within the hive by giving off pheromones.

Queen cage Small cage housing a young queen that is to be introduced into a colony or a nucleus.

Queen, marking the See *Year colors.*

Queen nucleus See page 30.

Queen substance (pheromone) A substance produced in the queen mandibular glands (see drawing on page 5) that affects the colony's activities.

Queen test See page 30.

Record cards All the activities inside the colony and all the maintenance chores performed by the beekeeper are entered on the record cards.

Requeening Replacing one queen with another (see page 34).

Robbing This behavior usually results from the beekeeper's carelessness. Bees "steal" the honey from other colonies. This can cause the demise of a colony.

Royal jelly A food substance produced by nurse bees (see *Nurse bee*) in their pharyngial glands and fed to larvae destined to become queens.

Scale colony If a hive is maintained on a scale, accurate observation of changes in weight is possible, which provides information on the abundance or scarcity of the honey flow.

Scent gland Also known as the Nassanoff gland, this gland is found on top of the abdomen of worker bees and produces a scent characteristic of that particular colony.

Shaking Moving a swarm from a box into the hive by giving the box a good shake or whack.

Smell, sense of The scent receptors of bees, which are located on the antennae, are very sensitive.

Smoke Smoke is blown at the bees to calm them.

Smoker A metal fire pot with bellows and a funnel to aim the smoke at a given target.

Smoker fuels Tobacco, punky wood, or dry pine needles.

Spring dwindling Population loss in the spring when old bees die faster than new ones emerge to take their place. Within reasonable limits this is a normal development.

Spur embedder A small brass wheel with grooved spurs used to mount the foundation into the wired frames.

Soy flour Pollen substitute (protein).

Sulfur Sulfur is used to kill diseased colonies.

Supersedure A colony replaces an old queen with a young one without swarming.

Swarm, artificial See page 33.

Swarming Natural division of a colony: Some of the bees move out of the hive (see *Swarm, prime* and *Afterswarm*).

Swarming impulse Bees are moved to swarm when the hive becomes congested; this occurs at the high point of the colony's population increase (see pages 6 and 26).

Swarm, prime The portion of the colony that leaves the hive with the old queen.

Uncapping Removal of the wax covers of combs filled with honey.

Vision Bees can distinguish colors. They are color blind to red but can see ultraviolet. Painting a part of the hive near the entrance in accordance with their color sense helps bees orientate themselves.

Water source A stream or other body of water or some watering device set up near the hives that supplies the bees with the water they need for processing food and regulating hive temperature.

Wax Worker bees excrete wax from glands located on the underside of the body between the abdominal segments.

Wax melter, solar A glass-covered box used for melting wax (old combs) by means of solar heat.

Waxmoth A parasite that destroys the combs.

Winter bees Bees that hatch in August and winter over.

Winter rest Bees survive the winter by contracting into a tight cluster.

Wiring foundation Stabilizing of the combs.

Worker Female bee with only partially developed ovaries; workers perform all the jobs, both inside and outside the hive, necessary for the survival of the colony (see pages 6 and 8).

Year colors To make it easier to find a queen and to keep track of her origin and age, she can be marked with a tiny disk attached to her thorax. The disks come in five different colors, each signifying a different year (see page 32).

Useful Literature and Addresses

Books

Butler, C. G., *The World of the Honeybee*, London: Collins, 1974.

Crane, Eva, ed., *Honey: A Comprehensive Survey*, New York: Crane, Russack & Co., 1975.

Dadant and Sons, eds., *The Hive and the Honey Bee*, Hamilton, IL: Dadant and Sons, 1975.

Dade, H. A., *Anatomy and Dissection of the Honeybee*, Kent, England: Bee Research Association Ltd., 1961.

Free, G. B., *Insect Pollination of Crops*, Washington, D.C.: Academic Press, 1970.

Hopper, Ted, *Guide to Bees and Honey*, Rodale Press Inc., Emmaus, PA, 1977.

Laidlaw, H. H., and Eckert, J. E., *Queens Rearing*, 2nd ed., Berkeley: University of California Press, 1962.

Lindauer, M., *Communication Among Social Bees*, New York: Atheneum, 1967.

Lovell, Harvey B., *Honey Plants Manual*, Medina, OH: The A. I. Root Co., Inc., 1956.

Michener, C. D., *The Social Behavior of Bees: A Comparative Study*, Cambridge, MA: Harvard University Press, 1974.

Morse, Roger A., *The Complete Guide to Beekeeping*, New York: E. P. Dutton Co., Inc., 1974.

Pellet, F. C., *American Honey Plants*, New York: Orange Judd & Co., 1947.

Proctor, Michael, and Yeo, Peter, *Pollination of Flowers*, New York: Taplinger, 1973.

Ribbands, C., *The Behavior and Social Life of Honeybees*, New York: Dover, 1953.

Root, A. I., *The ABC and XYZ of Bee Culture*, Medina, OH: The A. I. Root Co., 1978.

Snodgrass, R. E., *The Anatomy of the Honeybee*, Sausalito, CA: Comstock, 1956.

von Frische, Karl, *Bees: Their Vision, Chemical Senses and Language*, rev. ed., Ithaca, NY: Cornell University Press, 1971.

— *The Dance Language and Orientation of Bees*, Cambridge, MA: Harvard University Press, 1967.

Publications

American Bee Journal, Dadant & Sons, Inc., Hamilton, IL 62341.
Canadian Beekeeping, Box 128, Oronon, Ontario, Canada L0B 1M0.
Gleanings in Bee Culture, The A. I. Root Co., Box 706, Medina, OH 44256.

The USDA has issued a number of publications of interest to beekeepers, including *Beekeeping in the United States*, Agriculture Handbook No. 335 (Revised 1971), and S. E. McGregor, *Insect Pollination of Cultivated Plants*, Agriculture Handbook 496 (1976). These and other government publications are available from Superintendent of Documents, U.S. Government Printing Office, Washington, D.C. 20402.

Useful Literature and Addresses

Associations

American Beekeeping Federation, Rt. 1 Box 62, Cannon Falls, MN 55009.

American Honey Institute, 111 E. Wacker Drive, Chicago, IL 60601.

There are state beekeeping organizations in every state, many local beekeepers' associations, and regional organizations; please contact your local beekeepers, your county agricultural extension service, or your state department of agriculture.

Sources of Supply

Dadant & Sons, Inc., Hamilton, IL 62341.

A. I. Root Co., P.O. Box 706, Medina, OH 44256.

Both companies will accept mail orders and also have dealers throughout the United States whom beekeepers can visit for supplies, equipment, and advice.

Index

Index

Index

September, chores for, 50
Shaking, 65
Skeps, 20
Smell, sense of, 65
Smoke, 29, 65
Smoker, 65
Snowdrops, 46
Soy flour, 40, 65
Spring chores, 43
Spring dwindling, 65
Spring feeding, 25
Spur embedder, 25, 65
Stamping, 9
Stinging mechanism, 11
Stings, 13–14
Stonebrood, 57
Streptococcus pluton, 54
Sugar syrup, 25
Sulfur, 65
Sun, as reference point, 10
Supers, 26, 29
Supersedure, 7, 65
Supply sources, 67
Swarm, *C2*
Swarm catcher, 23
Swarming, 6–7, 47–48, 65
artificial swarm, 31-32
dealing with, 31

Swarming impulse, 65
Swarming prevention:
by colony expansion, 26
by colony relocation, 30
by creating artificial swarm, 33
by forming nucleus with a
queen, 30–31
by introducing queen into brood
nucleus, 34
by opening honey chamber or
adding supers, 26, 29
by shrinking colony, 29-30

Taxes, 15
Temperature, for survival, 7–8
Temporary hive, *27*
Time commitment, for
beekeeping, 14
Top-opening hive, 16
Training, for beekeeping, 13
Transport, 22–23
Transport floors, 22
Trough hive, 20

Uncapping, 65
Uncapping fork, *28*, 36

Varroa jakobsoni, 53

Varroatosis, 53
Venom, 11
Ventilation grid, 22
Virgin queen, 7
Viruses, 57
Vision, 65

Wag–tail dance, 9–10, *37*
Wasps, 11, 58
Water source, 65
Wax, 9, 51, 65
Wax melter (solar), 65
Waxmoths, 57, 65
White bees, 31
Wing clipping, of queen, 33
Winter:
chores for, 43
preparations for, 42–43
Winter bees, 65
Wintering over, 41
Winter rest, 65
Worker brood, 56
Workers, 5, 7, 12, *38*, 65

Year color, 32, 63
Yearly work cycle, 46–50

Zander hive, 20

Perfect for Pet Owners! ✓

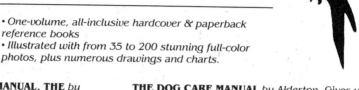